A Grain of Mustard

A Grain of Mustard

by JEANNE GARDNER

as told to BEATRICE MOORE

TRIDENT PRESS • NEW YORK

SBN: 671-27042-7
LIBRARY OF CONGRESS CATALOG CARD NUMBER: 72-92362
COPYRIGHT, ©, 1969, BY JEANNE GARDNER
ALL RIGHTS RESERVED. NO PART OF THIS BOOK MAY BE REPRODUCED IN ANY FORM WITHOUT PERMISSION IN WRITING FROM THE PUBLISHER, EXCEPT BY A REVIEWER WHO MAY QUOTE BRIEF PASSAGES IN A REVIEW TO BE PRINTED IN A MAGAZINE OR NEWSPAPER.
PUBLISHED SIMULTANEOUSLY IN THE UNITED STATES AND CANADA BY TRIDENT PRESS, A DIVISION OF SIMON & SCHUSTER, INC., 630 FIFTH AVENUE, NEW YORK, N.Y. 10020
PRINTED IN THE UNITED STATES OF AMERICA

To my mother's family, who taught me the meaning of faith, and to all those people who have believed in me and in my life's work.

Introduction

In the course of my life I have met some remarkable persons, but none more remarkable than Jeanne Gardner.

This is her story, and I commend it to all—the erudite and the unlettered, the doubters and the believers, and especially to those who are open-minded and sensitive to the beauty and mystery of our lives.

It will be by her extraordinary gifts of prophecy and clairvoyance that Jeanne will be chiefly known.

But those of us who have been privileged to know her personally have been enchanted by something more— the invincible power of her personality.

For Jeanne is a child of complete, primitive faith—a fresh flower in the technological desert of the sophisticated twentieth century.

Her visions and voices have enabled her to predict innumerable events that have subsequently been borne out in fact.

But her simple, unquestioning, childlike faith in these visions has enabled her to accomplish the impossible, to move mountains.

Famous and powerful personages of our times have felt the warmth and benign magnetism of Jeanne. When she has needed help to pursue the great spiritual goal which

A Grain of Mustard

she has accepted as her life work, the help has always been provided—in ways stranger than fiction.

It is all written here, as Jeanne tells it, simply, movingly, without sensationalism or embellishment.

I do not purport to be a literary critic. I can only say that the story of Jeanne's prophecies and clairvoyant gifts will absorb you, and the imprint of the rare personality of this child of faith will remain with you always.

HAROLD E. HUGHES
United States Senator from Iowa

Foreword

Jeanne Gardner has told her story like it is. This is an honest account of a woman whose love of God comes through with every word she speaks and in every detail of her existence. Her dedication to build a Cathedral of Prayer is an unmatched devotion to God and to her fellow man. She has proved beyond a doubt that "faith the size of a mustard seed can move mountains."

MAHALIA JACKSON

chapter 1

EASTER, 1961, was a day I shall never forget. My mother had been taken from me a few weeks earlier, and I was still deeply saddened by my loss. To make matters worse, our community had been hit by a snowstorm, the worst in memory for that time of year. But it was that Easter that changed the course of my life and prompted me to carry on my mother's dream of building a Cathedral on the outskirts of our home town, Elkins, West Virginia.

It was on the night before the holiday that I looked out of the window and noticed that the snow was still falling heavily. Easter Sunday wouldn't seem like Easter Sunday at all. I picked up the evening paper and sat down in the rocker to read. But I couldn't concentrate. As I sat there, my head fell backward and a distant voice spoke to me, telling me to go the next morning to the Memorial Gardens where my mother was buried to witness the most glorious sunrise I had ever seen. I forced myself to sit upright and fearfully looked across the room. There was no one in the room but me. Was I losing my mind? I knew what the weather was like at that moment, and I had

A Grain of Mustard

heard the forecast of continued snow. There could be no glorious sunrise, yet I was certain I had heard the voice, or at least I thought I was certain.

I raced to the telephone and called my mother's sister. Aunt Bess was well aware of the gift of prophecy that had been my mother's, and she herself had visions from time to time. Maybe she could help me. She listened patiently while I spelled out the details of the preceding fifteen minutes; then she spoke to me in comforting tones.

"Jeanne, if it will make you happy to go to Memorial Gardens at five o'clock tomorrow morning, I'll go with you."

I felt somewhat better. There was at least one person who didn't believe I was crazy.

Later, after saying goodnight to my family and preparing for bed, I prayed as I had never prayed before:

"Dear God, please give me a sign. Let me know if I am imagining things or if I am to continue my mother's work. I am tormented. I don't know which way to turn. Please give me proof . . . proof that I am not mentally unbalanced, or proof that You are by my side. Only You can create a glorious sunrise through this snowstorm. I will be waiting." I continued my prayers, then crept into bed, not to sleep but to wait for 4 A.M.

My husband was bitterly opposed to my starting out at that dark hour in a snowstorm, but my aunt was staunch and ready to go when I called for her. Moreover, two other members of my family joined us for the expedition.

We arrived at the Memorial Gardens in plenty of time,

parked the car, and waited. After what seemed like an eternity, the clouds to our right parted and a ray of light shone through. We all sat quietly, expectantly, but nothing further happened. Another half hour passed, and we agreed that the trip was wasted, so I started the motor and turned the car toward town.

When I had driven about a mile down the road, I heard that distant voice once again, telling me to pull off to the side of the road. I did so immediately, much to the surprise of everyone who was with me. But before there was time for them to question my actions, the miracle occurred. Directly ahead of us, just above the crest of the mountain, the clouds parted and the sun came toward us like a ball of fire. It seemed as though it were suspended on a string. It danced and it twirled, it moved forward and drifted back. None of us in the car was able to grasp what was happening. It was unbelievable. Finally my aunt spoke.

"Jeanne dear," she said, "you've seen your glorious sunrise. Do you feel better now? Do you know what you have to do?"

"Not yet, Aunt Bess. I want to see a rainbow. God gave Noah a rainbow, and I have asked Him for the same. Let's wait and see."

We continued to watch as the sun played games with us. Then, magically, the clouds surrounding the sun took the form of a stairway, and each step was a different color. It was the most beautiful rainbow any of us had ever seen.

We drove back to Elkins then, my mother's family chattering among themselves, and I quietly content but over-

A Grain of Mustard

whelmed by the knowledge that I had a tremendous task ahead of me. I didn't know then how long it would take me or what obstacles I would encounter along the way, but I knew that someday, somehow, the Cathedral of Prayer my mother had envisioned would be a reality. I knew I could do it now.

"Faith the size of a mustard seed can move mountains."

Through my experiences over the past eight years, from the moment I knew that my mother was dying and realized that I might have to carry on her mission, I have acquired faith. What, you may ask, is faith? Even now I cannot explain it. I know it is a spirit that is all around me, a feeling of energy, a force that directs my mind and body and still leaves me free.

For eight years I have struggled, negotiated, haggled, begged, and cajoled all for one purpose: to build the Cathedral of Prayer. This year the ground will be broken, and in 1970 the vision that was first my mother's and then mine will be realized.

I cannot tell you why my mother and I were chosen for this work. My mother was a rolling stone who married three times. She had no fixed religion, no constant faith.

And who am I, Jeanne Gardner, daughter of this rolling-stone mother and a father whom I wouldn't know if our paths were to cross today? Jeanne Gardner, to the city-bred a hillbilly, to the people of my town an ordinary housewife and mother of three. I have seen very little of the world, yet through my visions and the Voice I have been able to prophesy Khrushchev's downfall and Mikoyan's rise to power, the assassination of President Kennedy and later of his brother Robert. I have been able to help patients declared hopeless by their doctors and to save people who, if they had carried out their plans, would have died accidental deaths. The details surrounding these events will be spelled out as my story unfolds.

I know that I am a very small instrument in a blueprint that was drawn long before my time and that my responsibility to build a Cathedral for all faiths was predestined.

My mother told me in 1960, a year before she died, that I would one day have our story published. I am not well educated, I am not a writer, and I could not believe then that my mother knew what she was saying. Yet here I am, having been moved by that unexplainable force to set down the experiences that led to this project. Since the members of my mother's family play important roles in the story, I'll begin by introducing them.

I was born May 11, 1930, to Daisy Elizabeth Hanger Francis and Thurmond Sherwood Francis in the bedroom of my Grandmother Hanger's house in Elkins, West Virginia. It was Mother's Day, and a miraculous day for my mother and for me because I was one of the few surviving blue babies of that era. The important thing is that I did live and that I believe I was destined by God to live for a very special reason.

My mother had married my father on impulse when she was seventeen years old. I was born eleven months later before they had really adjusted to each other. Neither was ready for marriage nor for the responsibilities of parenthood.

When I was three months old, we moved to the home of my father's parents, in Henrietta, Oklahoma. I do not recall what the household situation was at that time, because I was too young. But I have been told that my parents' marriage came to an end when I was eighteen months old. The separation followed a year of bitter arguments that stemmed from my father's drinking and endless affairs with other women.

Grandma and Grandpa Francis tried in every way to convince my mother to remain in Oklahoma because they loved her and me, but my mother wouldn't hear of it. She packed our few belongings and brought me back to Elkins to the home of her parents.

My grandmother's house was a typical country frame house and was painted yellow. Today, with an ache in my heart, I hear some of our townspeople refer to it as "the old yellow house." The ache is in my heart because I have a lifetime of memories in that house, some good, some bad, but to me, that "old yellow house" is the reason for my existence and for my purpose.

Grandma's house was a haven for all of her children and their offspring. There were usually more people staying there than the house could comfortably hold, but they were always welcome.

At the time my mother brought me to Grandma's in 1932, my bachelor uncle, Mike, was living there, as well as two of my mother's sisters, Aunt Laura and Aunt Bess. Life was far from easy. My grandfather was a carpenter who worked long hours under the most difficult conditions for very little pay. He never complained, however, and even expressed his gratitude for the privilege of being able to keep his brood together. Jobs for women during those Depression days were out of the question, and jobs for men were few and far between.

When I was two years old, my grandfather died, and the burden of responsibility fell on the shoulders of my Uncle Mike. Since Mike earned only seventeen dollars every two weeks, those of us who "boarded" at Grandma's were often dependent upon kind neighbors who shared their food with us.

Mama, who had taken to the road to find work, sent Grandma whatever change she had left from her pay, but it was pitifully little.

How many times I sat down to stew and gingerbread during my first five years I cannot say. But whenever I would look pleadingly at my grandmother for more food, she always had the same comment: "Let us thank God we have this."

My grandmother was confined to a wheelchair, and she had to cling to the furniture for support when she did the housework, but her spirit was as strong as her limbs were weak. She didn't get to church regularly, but she prayed a lot. Her prayers were not the kind that you hear in the pulpit, but more like conversations with a good friend.

Cruel though it seems today, I used to ridicule Grandma

A Grain of Mustard

when she declared that she was a prophet. Sometimes she would predict the arrival of a relative from the North on Thursday at three o'clock, or a snowstorm at a time of year when snow was most unlikely. The fact is, however, that her predictions were always right, and despite the fact that Grandma insisted that this clairvoyance was a gift from God, those of us who lived with her, except for Uncle Mike, laughed and called her lucky. Little did I realize then that my grandmother did indeed have the gift of prophecy and that I would one day inherit that gift.

Fortunately, childhood spares us from understanding hardship. We may be deprived, but we are too young to be saddened by it. There are too many simple things for young hearts to enjoy.

In the evenings at Grandma's, following the stew and gingerbread, all of us would gather around in the living room for family entertainment. None of Grandma's children had been given musical training, but they all took to their instruments as naturally as bees to honey. My uncle played the guitar and piano, my aunts played the piano, and all of us sang. My mother's visits were, of course, special occasions for me. I thought she was more talented than the rest, and in my childish fantasies she was a glamorous vaudeville star.

No, life was not sad. What I lacked in food and the necessities of life was more than adequately compensated through love and the happiness that comes from being with good friends. I can remember looking across the room at Grandma with the feeling that my heart would burst with devotion, and I still am filled with joy when I think of how my grandmother returned my affection.

In 1935, when the WPA came into being, my Uncle Mike found somewhat better employment, and for the first time in my life I tasted the food that most people had been eating every day.

I entered the First Ward School in Elkins when I was six, and although I was poor and ashamed of being the only one in the class to wear long black stockings, I felt welcome. I loved my teacher and tried every way I knew to show my heartfelt gratitude for the friendship of my classmates.

The family entertainment in the evenings continued, and before I was eight, I had learned to tap dance. With my frend Doralee Grimm, I entered amateur contests in and around our town, and many times we came home with the first prize. I think now that one of the greatest moments of my childhood was winning the loving cup at the local theater.

There were times when I longed to have the clothes and toys and treats that other children had; there were times when my childish mind questioned my circumstances. On these occasions I would go to Grandma. She was my rock and my comfort. Her reassuring words, "Thank God you have as much as you have," her loving smile and her arms around me were like a tonic.

When I finished the second grade, my mother took me back to Oklahoma for a visit with Grandmother and Grandfather Francis, and they persuaded her to let me remain with them for a year. I attended the Henrietta school, and my grandparents also arranged for me to take elocution lessons. It was an experience for which I shall be forever grateful, because it transformed me from a socially shy child into one who was able to respond to people. I was happy with my father's parents, but my mother insisted that I return to Elkins at the end of the year. It was another wrench for me. I loved those dear people, and I knew that they loved me. Yet, once back in Elkins, I was caught up in the family life at Grandma Hanger's, and my year in Henrietta melted into a pleasant memory.

Once more I joined my class at the First Ward School, and life took on a familiar routine. Uncle Mike continued to support the crowd at Grandma's, although the number was reduced by the marriage of my Aunt Bess. Mama was off again, working first at one job, then at another, and popping back to Elkins every now and then to see me. Even when my mother was away, I knew that she loved me and that her absence was the result of her concern for my welfare. She couldn't work and take care of me, too. At Grandma's, I was passed around like a community doll. One person dressed me, another fixed my long hair in finger curls, and all those present made certain that no harm came to me.

Grandma continued her conversations with the Divine Power and added to our daily pleasure with gems of wisdom and an occasional prediction which, oddly enough, always came to pass at the precise moment and in the manner that she had prophesied. I considered it vastly entertaining and used Grandma as my central character in the stories I would tell to my classmates.

We were still dreadfully poor, but I wasn't discontented. There is something about a small town—our town—that makes money secondary.

Because the town is small and there are very few recreational facilities, the people depend on each other for entertainment—visits to neighbors, community picnics, and trips to the national parks. Our activities follow the seasons . . . sledding parties in winter followed by steaming bowls of soup or chili at a neighbor's house . . . barbecues in spring and summer and swimming parties. Autumn is particularly beautiful, for then the valley is ablaze with color. The awe-inspiring sight attracts people from all over the country, and many attend our Mountain Forest Festival. For this occasion, the townspeople of Elkins become one family with each member doing his share to make the Festival a success.

I do not believe that I am unusually sentimental or more filled with community pride than the next person. I can only say that in this tiny corner of nowhere there is beauty, there is peace, and there is happiness. That is why I am so grateful to have been blessed with the task of building a Cathedral in a place where God's presence is so apparent.

chapter 2

You may get the impression from my frequent reference to God and from the fact that I am involved with the erection of a religious center that I am deeply religious. In the traditional sense, believe me, I am not. I changed churches as often as homes, and there were long intervals when I didn't attend church at all. Yet I know from the experiences I have had that God's presence is everywhere and that, as the popular song tells us, "He's got the whole world in His hand."

I believe now that it was through His divine intervention that my mother met Paul Bernard, a railroad stockman. Paul was considerably older than Mama, with a quiet, unassuming manner that was as comfortable as an old shoe. He had never been married and still lived at home with his parents, who treated him as their little boy. But he was completely smitten by my mother's good looks, her beautiful red hair, and her disarming personality, and after a very brief courtship they were married. At last, I thought, I would have a home. Unfortunately, the arrangement was short-lived.

Paul was good to me and welcomed me with the same affection he would have given his own child. But while his devotion to my mother was unfailing, he couldn't sever the old family ties. His mother, father, and sisters wanted him at their house every night. These demands on his time and their criticism of my mother's domestic abilities soon became points of contention between Paul and Mama. Mama sought an outlet by taking a job at the depot newsstand. The job meant that they could spend even less time together, and Mama, in her old irresponsible fashion, made matters worse by stopping at a club with friends on her way from the depot. Her absences from home became more frequent until Paul told her that he couldn't continue with the marriage.

This put Mama and me right back where we'd started, with no home and no money. Instead of going to Grandma's, this time we took a small apartment in Elkins. I was not yet twelve, too young to work, and the jobs that my mother could handle were scarce. There were many nights when we went to bed hungry. Somehow, though, my darling Uncle Mikey often seemed to turn up at the eleventh hour. On a number of occasions when we had reached the depths of despair and wondered where we were going to get food for the following day, Uncle Mike appeared at the door with a sack of groceries in his arms. But the situation went from bad to worse, and the landlord got progressively louder in his demands for the rent.

Then one day my mother received a letter from her sister, Bess, who was living in Cumberland, Maryland. Bess

A Grain of Mustard

now had two small children, but wanted to accept a job in a defense plant. She asked Mama if she would come to Cumberland with me and take care of the children. It seemed like a logical solution, so once again we packed our meager belongings and made our way to a new home.

It was while we were in Cumberland that Paul Bernard came to pay Mama a visit. He told her he realized that their separation had been caused by his weakness and begged her to resume their marriage. So that he would not be influenced by his family again, he offered to transfer to Cumberland. My mother knew what a sacrifice this was and she told Paul she would be glad to have him back. They parted that day with his promise to make the necessary transfer arrangements so that they could take up their lives where they had left off. Once again I looked forward to a home. The reconciliation didn't come to pass, however, because when Paul returned to Elkins to tell his family of his intention, they preyed upon his soft disposition and convinced him that he should remain with them. My mother was heartbroken, and the pain showed clearly on her face. It was the first time that I observed her as an older person rather than as an ageless friend. Paul Bernard finally divorced Mama, and with him completely out of her life, she once again became a rolling stone.

I was returned to Grandma's house in Elkins and enrolled in junior high school. Strangely enough, the eternal conflicts at home in no way cast a shadow on my school life. I was actively interested in the school program, participated in girls' athletics, served as a cheerleader, and was a majorette with the school band. Grandma Hanger had a tremendous influence on my attitude. Out of the bigness of her heart, she tried to compensate for the parental love I lacked, by helping me develop into the kind of person who would appreciate what I had and not dwell on the things I didn't have. She epitomized life's three greatest treasures: faith, hope, and charity. With her as an example, I learned patience, and her many sacrifices and kindnesses taught me a great deal about responsibilities for others.

Grandma continued her daily conversations with God, and during my teen-age years I began to pay attention to her predictions. I turned to her because I noticed that, more often than not, her guidance took me in the right direction. Pursuing a path I chose for myself often led to distress, sometimes to disaster. I began to understand that Grandma would always shelter me from harm if she could and that I could rely on her prophecies. The things that happened to me weren't always good, but Grandma would tell me philosophically that we had to learn to take the bitter with the better.

During the time that I had been living with my mother, my Uncle Mike had married, and now he, his wife, and their three children occupied Grandma's house. I was fourteen, old enough to care for myself. I learned to sew and made many of my own clothes. After school I had jobs that provided me with spending money.

Grandma's house was overcrowded. There was too much conversation in the evenings, too much tumult and excite-

A *Grain of Mustard*

ment with the young children. But Grandma never complained. Her health was declining rapidly, and Mike's wife, Hazel, was heaven-sent. She helped with the housework and kept the family together, never giving any indication that she had taken over, and thus permitting Grandma to feel that she was still at the helm. Grandma continued her prayers and prophecies, but often they were from her bed.

My mother meantime had rambled up and down the East Coast, finally settling in a job at an ammunition plant in Radford, Virginia. There she enjoyed, at last, a salary that enabled her to save, and while she saved, she thought about her future. She had always been impeccable, had always taken a great deal of pride in her dress and in her hair. She was interested in hair styling and decided to take a course in beauty culture. After having obtained her license, she found work in a beauty shop. This spurred her ambition, and after a year's time she was able to open a place of her own. She discovered a talent for business of which she had not been aware. Her salon thrived. She sold the small shop and bought a larger one. I was happy for Mama but longed secretly for her to return to Elkins and to me, knowing in my heart that I was wishing for the impossible.

When Aunt Bess and Uncle Herman moved from Cumberland back to Elkins, they took me to live with them. I was then a junior in high school. It was with mixed emotions that I left Grandma's house. I felt that I wanted to be near her and return some of the many kindnesses she had shown me, yet I knew that I was the one person in that overcrowded house who was dispensable, because about this time my Aunt Laura had separated from her husband and she and her daughter had returned to Grandma's. My room was needed for them.

So once more, at age fourteen, I moved.

Fourteen is a painful year at best. You are no longer a child, but neither are you accepted as an adult. Disturbed by the plain process of growing up, I was also bothered by a number of nagging questions. Why had my father never acknowledged my existence? Why was I constantly being uprooted? How could my mother be content in one place knowing that I was in another? Why was there so much confusion and change in my grandmother's house? Why had my Aunt Laura left her husband?

The last question bothered me more than I can say. I was old enough to realize how important it is to have a wholesome family life, with a man at the head of the household. My aunt and uncle had seemed happy together, they shared the devotion of their child, and they had acquired more material possessions than most people of their ages. Yet the one thing that is supposed to bind people together had torn them apart: religion. Through friends Aunt Laura had developed an interest in a new Pentecostal Church. Her husband was bitterly opposed to her attendance there. He challenged her to choose between the Pentecostal Church and him. Aunt Laura selected the church. I was disillusioned, confused, tormented by this paradox of life. Where was God? Where was this Divine Power of which I had been told by Grandma? Why didn't

A Grain of Mustard

He look out for people like my Aunt Laura and my mother? Why didn't He put His arms around kids like me who were batted from pillar to post?

I lived through those growing pains, but not before I'd moved a few more times. While I was living with Aunt Bess and Uncle Herman, my Uncle Luke and Aunt Hannah came into the picture. Their daughter was no longer living at home, and they decided among themselves that I would have better care at their house.

Aunt Hannah's personality was far from carefree. She was demanding and insisted that her demands be met with no alterations. I had an after-school job at Neal's Drugstore, and my hours there ended at half past nine, sometimes quarter to ten. If I was delayed by having to wait on one more customer or by a conversation with a friend on my way home, I was locked out because Aunt Hannah locked the door promptly at 10 P.M. No excuse was acceptable, and there was no deviation from the rule. Moreover, she would call at the drugstore and give me a list of items to bring home. By the time the week was out, I had nothing left of my pay. When I turned to Grandma for consolation, I found that Aunt Hannah had already been there with tales of untruth about my indolence, insolence, and misconduct. Life was worse than it had ever been. The only hope lay in graduating from high school. Then, I thought, I will have a full-time job and a life I can call my own.

Before I graduated, however, I went back to Grandma's to live and thrived once again on her faith and her wisdom.

When I finished school, I had more than a diploma to carry with me. I had the memory of good friendships, team activities, and work on the school newspaper. While my family life had always taken me on an uphill road, my school life had been stimulating. I had missed many things because I lacked the money to participate, but there were still a great many experiences that I had enjoyed.

chapter 3

FOLLOWING my graduation, I continued to work at the drugstore, but life seemed somewhat easier. I had leisure time now for social and community activities.

I was an attractive teen-ager and, like most attractive people, I was not lacking in friendships. There were the usual Saturday night dates and Sunday picnics, but I had made up my mind that I would never act hastily as far as the opposite sex was concerned. I did not want to repeat my mother's mistake and spend the rest of my life regretting it. World War II had ended and a lot of the boys I had known in high school were coming back from the service. Some of them wanted to find wives and settle down immediately. Aware of this, I assumed an attitude of aloofness that was really not characteristic of me. I did not want to be caught in a web that was inescapable. Fate, however, defied my decision.

One Sunday I joined a group of friends for a swimming party at the State park. While we were there, we met other people our own age, and among them was a young man by the name of Harold Gardner. I remembered him from school, although he had been a couple of grades ahead of me. His nickname was "Spider," and he had been a high school hero, a basketball star who made the All-State championship team. Spider had just returned from military service and hadn't been back in Elkins very long. Before the day ended, he had invited me to a dance the following Saturday. Torn between my desire to see him again and the pact I had made with myself, I told him I'd think about it. A few days later he telephoned me at the drugstore, and I enthusiastically agreed to attend the dance. That was the beginning of our two-year courtship, and on March 26, 1948, we were married in a service at the Evangelistical United Brethren Church.

The church made no real difference to me. I had been born to Presbyterians, christened in the Baptist Church, had attended the Church of God with my grandmother, and had been bounced from one creed to another. The important thing to me was being married in the sight of God and making my husband happy.

Can you imagine what this union meant? Jeanne Francis, who had never known the feeling of belonging to one person, was at last going to be united with one special being who loved her. Jeanne Francis, who had never known the feeling of real roots, was at last going to have a place to call home.

My wedding day was beautiful in every way. Because it meant so much to me, I wanted every detail to be perfect. I made my wedding gown after exhaustive deliberation. Some of my attendants were in borrowed clothes, but the

A Grain of Mustard

assemblage looked like a picture in the Sunday rotogravure.

Without consulting me, my aunt and Grandma Francis decided that my father, who had never participated in my support, should be contacted through the courts and asked to furnish a sum that would help me in establishing my home. This apparently was accomplished with no real difficulty, and I started my married life with a thousand dollars for furniture and without the headaches of monthly payments.

Spider and I lived in a five-room apartment over his mother's garage, and, dreary though it may sound to the average housewife, I cleaned and scrubbed, dusted and cooked with unflagging enthusiasm. This home was indeed my prize. Only a person who had nothing in his early life could appreciate how much every little knickknack meant to me.

Busy though I was, I still found my way to Grandma's each and every day. By this time she was bedridden most of the time, but never downcast. Grandma could be suffering acute pain and still manage a cheerful word and a smile. Frequently I would talk to her about my mother. She knew how much I had missed that important relationship, and we prayed together that my mother would come home.

Mama, at this point, was doing very well. She had sold her beauty shops because the long hours of standing had aggravated her varicose veins. Through a motel owner she knew in Georgia, she then found employment as a motel manager, and later, through acquaintances she made in the business, she was able to lease a place of her own in Florida. Her situation was better than ever, and she was less inclined to return to Elkins than she had been before. She had a staff of employees to maintain the rooms and coffee shop, and for the first time in her life she had some free time to do the things she loved. Since music had always given her much enjoyment, she devoted her spare time to writing songs, never with a view to seeking publication, but solely for the gratification she derived from putting her thoughts into lyrical form.

This was something she had always had a nagging compulsion to do. She often said that a song, with lyrics, would pop into her head. She wouldn't have time or facilities to write down what she heard, and the song would "get away."

Now she had the time, and she looked for songs to come to her. It was vastly fulfilling to be able to doodle around on the piano with a tune that haunted her.

I corresponded with my mother, and from time to time she would come for a hasty visit.

She had been married for the third time to a man by the name of Henry Crawford, who, to the best of my knowledge, was working for the U.S. government. She was widowed shortly afterward when he met his death in a bomb explosion in Venezuela.

On September 25, 1949, Spider and I had our first child, a son whom we christened Robert Morton. Bobby added joy to our lives and was the kind of baby that inspires a married couple to want a larger family. I prayed for an-

A Grain of Mustard

other child, and on June 10, 1951, my prayers were answered with a beautiful baby girl whom we named Pamela.

In 1952 we learned of a house being built in an area of Elkins where I had sledded as a child. We drove out to see the place and found a small frame house surrounded by trees, trees, and more trees. To some, it might have looked hopeless. To me, it looked like a mansion. I wanted it desperately for our family, but, with the expenses of daily living and maintaining our two babies, we had not yet accumulated enough money for a down payment. Spider asked me to be patient, and I tried to be, but I couldn't get the house out of my mind. I had heard that the government had established a plan known as a Direct Loan, in which no down payment on the part of the purchaser was required. I made inquiries through business people in town, only to learn that nobody in Elkins had been able to qualify for this type of loan. But I couldn't give up that easily. Without telling Spider, I corresponded with the F.H.A., and, much to my pleasure and surprise, I found that the picture was encouraging. The loan was granted, and in June, 1952, we moved into our house in the wilderness.

There was much to be done to the house and yard, and Spider and I worked with fervent dedication. Our backs ached, and our hands were sore, but our hearts were light because we were two young people on our way to seeing a dream come true. I loved the responsibility of caring for my home and looking after my little ones. Every now and then, when neighbors would be refurnishing a room or getting rid of a table or a chair, I would tell them I'd be glad to take anything they didn't want. With great glee, I would then drag these "treasures" home to decide where they could best be used. I painted, I tied springs and upholstered, and I derived great satisfaction from creating an object of beauty from someone else's discard.

At last, I thought, I know the true meaning of contentment.

This feeling came to a screeching halt in 1954 when, as I stood in my living room one day in May, I was suddenly stricken with a hemorrhage from the female organs. I ran from the house and found my friend and neighbor, Minnie Albright, who drove me to our family doctor. He examined me carefully and, after what seemed like an eternity, confronted me with the startling news that he believed I had cancer. He urged me to go directly to a surgeon and made an immediate appointment. The surgeon, after examining me, concurred with my doctor's diagnosis and recommended that I sign in at the hospital immediately.

My thoughts fled to my two small children at home. Who would take care of them on such short notice? My friend Minnie, still at my side, volunteered. She assured me as she left me at the hospital that she and her husband would move into my house and would stay as long as they were needed. So, with my mind at rest, I registered at the hospital and put myself in the hands of the medical professionals. Biopsy followed biopsy. Three times the reports came back negative, yet the doctors were unable to determine what the problem really was or how to solve it.

A Grain of Mustard

Because I was only twenty-four, they ruled out a hysterectomy. Instead, they prescribed medication which I continued to take long after I returned home.

Through all this difficult time I had a constant nagging desire to see my mother. Yet something inside me would not yield to the idea of letting her know what was happening or asking her to come to see me. It seemed to me that it would be too great a sacrifice to impose on her. She was successful now. She owned her own business and was doing well.

Without my knowledge, the members of my family got in touch with Mama and told her that my condition had been diagnosed as cancer and that there was still some doubt. This news changed the entire course of my mother's life, and for the first time in her forty-three years on earth, she knew what she really wanted. She sold her motel, left the past behind, and returned to Elkins to be near me and my family.

chapter 4

To ME, Mama's presence was worth any pain and suffering that I had endured. At last I had my mother. Having her close was all that I had ever wanted. Being able to see her and talk with her was more effective treatment than any doctor had prescribed.

At the time I was discharged from the hospital, I had been told that I could never have another child, but I had been too sick to give it much thought. However, with Mama home and my condition improving, I began to reflect on the pattern of my life and to wonder why so many of my hopes had been dashed by circumstances beyond my control.

What I didn't realize was that adversity can often produce beneficial effects. Despite the doctors' verdict I learned early in 1956 that I was pregnant again. I was delighted, even though the doctors were concerned that I could not carry the baby for the full term or that if I did, one of us would die. Somehow I knew in my heart that everything would be all right. It was a difficult nine months during which I spent many weeks in the hos-

A Grain of Mustard

pital, having blood test after blood test. Since I had an Rh factor, there was ever-present concern for my life and for the life of the child I was carrying. Toward the end of the pregnancy I was prepared for the fact that the baby would probably be stillborn; there had been no evidence of heartbeat for several days. However, on August 26, 1956, my precious Barry saw the light of day, and we took comfort with each other. I know that God put Barry on this earth for a special reason, and part of that reason has already been revealed, as I will describe later.

Immediately following Barry's birth, the doctors decided to pack me with antibiotics, and this treatment was responsible for the restoration of my health for the next several years.

Once more I assumed the role of wife and mother with great heart and ambition. And having Mama close by was an added source of pleasure.

The years of constant struggle and final achievement had given my mother the desire to remain active. She talked of building a motel in Elkins, but one day we heard that there was a drive-in restaurant for sale. She already had some restaurant experience in conjunction with her motel operation, and the prospect of buying an established business and then perhaps building a motel around it appealed to her.

We went down to look at Rock's Snack Bar and liked what we saw. We negotiated with the owners, and before long Mama and I found ourselves the proprietors of the Casa Sands Drive-In Restaurant. The chef who had been at my mother's motel in Florida came to work for us, and the word soon spread that we were serving unusually tasty food at very popular prices. Mama and I worked hard, and the business prospered.

Mama's attitude was a complete reversal of her younger days. She was as contented at being back in Elkins as she had been discontented before. She was no longer seeking greener pastures, and she seemed to need her mother as much as I had always felt I needed mine. As for Grandma, she was beside herself with joy at having Mama back. She thrived on Mama's daily visits and thanked God that we were at last a family.

I don't know whether it started as a means of making Grandma happy or as a way of acquiring her own faith, but my mother began to pray with Grandma and no longer scoffed at Grandma's predictions and prophecies.

But the lighter side of my mother's personality had not faded. She still loved her music and hummed or sang the songs she had written as she went about her chores.

One day a stranger came into the restaurant. He said he was in a dreadful hurry and asked if we had a phone. Mama pointed to the public telephone and continued her work. When the man had completed his phone call, he thanked Mama and started out the door, but Mama asked him to wait for just a moment. She confessed that she had overheard his conversation and had heard him identify himself as a representative of Capitol Records. He acknowledged that he was, and while he still appeared to be in a hurry, he was patient with Mama and listened to her

A Grain of Mustard

story. She told the gentleman that she had written several songs as a hobby and that while she was in Florida a representative of RCA had heard her playing one of her songs and had suggested that she take it to Perry Como. She asked the Capitol Records man if he would listen to the demonstration record that she had made and give her the benefit of his opinion. The man told her that he had an appointment but offered to come back when he had finished with his business.

True to his word, he returned that night for dinner and Mama played the record. He liked what he heard and agreed that it was a perfect song for Como. He suggested that Mama have a new demonstration record made with a more modern arrangement and told her how to go about making contact at RCA. He was unusually helpful, and before he left that night, he offered to do what he could at Capitol if we were unsuccessful at RCA. Mama was in seventh heaven.

She was sitting there thinking about what had transpired when Mr. Golden, an acquaintance from Clarksburg, came in for dinner. When he asked what was new, Mama really told him. She regaled him with the whole long tale from the beginning and, strangely enough, Mr. Golden thought he could be of assistance. He said he knew someone who might be willing to cut the demonstration record for her. A week or so later, when Mr. Golden came through Elkins again, he stopped in to say that the musical conductor of WPDX in Clarksburg would be willing to lend his services, but that it would cost two-hundred and fifty dollars.

Two-hundred and fifty dollars at that moment seemed like an enormous fortune to us. All the money we had was tied up in the business. But the possibility of hearing a brilliant star like Perry Como sing one of Mama's songs was too much for us. We sat there long after Mr. Golden left and thought about the people we knew who might let us have the money for the project.

My Uncle Mikey's father-in-law had a bit of money at that time, and we decided to approach him. It didn't require much persuasion on our part. He gave us the money with a free heart and a blessing, assuring us that he was happy to play a part in my mother's recognition as a songwriter.

We made an appointment at the radio station in Clarksburg with the musical director, Joe DeRosa, and felt that we were on our way. I can still remember the expression of joy on my mother's face as she listened to her song being recorded by a live orchestra. We returned to Elkins and to the responsibilities of our restaurant, but now we were preoccupied with getting Mama's song published. Mama was already mentally spending the royalties to build a motel behind the restaurant, and we were both as enthusiastic as two kids on a picnic.

Mama talked to everybody who came in, hoping that the law of averages would bring her someone who could be of help. One day a local disc jockey happened in for lunch. Mama took him aside and, after giving him the complete background, asked him if he knew anyone in New York who was in the music business. He said he did and that he

A Grain of Mustard

would be glad to put us in touch. This led us to an agent and brought us perilously close to disaster.

After an exchange of correspondence and a phone call or two, the agent informed us that he could better generate Perry Como's interest if the song was recorded by the Ray Charles Singers, but that this would cost three thousand dollars. Our desire to get the song to Como was still strong, but the possibility of putting our hands on three thousand dollars threw us into a complete state of frustration.

Mama seemed quieter for the next couple of days. Then one day she rushed up to me in the restaurant and told me she had a feeling that she must go to Grandma's house right away. Since my mother didn't drive a car, I took her over. Grandma lay in her bed. My Uncle Mike and Aunt Laura were with her. Mother burst into the room and sat down in a rocking chair. She explained that she had come as though driven by a force. Then suddenly her head fell back and her eyes closed. She tried to open them but couldn't. It was on this occasion that my mother had her first vision. It was in three parts. The first showed Mama a check for three thousand dollars, although she could not see the signature that was affixed. The second part was Mama's song printed on sheet music. And the third scene was of a beautiful orchard, shaded by green leaves suffused with misty light. Accompanying the vision was a voice that said, "When the green leaves fall from the trees, the land will be yours." Mama's eyes opened then and she looked around, stunned.

Aunt Laura grabbed Mama's wrist and asked, "Daisy, what's wrong?" My mother replied that it was nothing. The experience was too new, too strange for her to want to impart it to anyone. But she had hardly answered Laura when her head fell back and the vision was repeated exactly as it had been a few moments before. This time, when she regained her composure, she revealed to us what she had experienced. My grandmother was overcome with ecstasy, and Mike and Laura looked at Mama with love and understanding, because they had been aware for many years that Grandma's gift had passed to her offspring.

Mama and I rode back to the restaurant, amazed at what had transpired, but wondering who would be responsible for the three-thousand-dollar check or if, in fact, we could trust the vision. In my secret heart I thought Mama's mind might be playing tricks on her because of her raging desire to achieve her purpose, but I said nothing.

Back at the drive-in, we set about our respective chores, but we were interrupted by a phone call from Laura who was insistent that we return to Grandma's immediately. Recognizing the urgency in her voice, we jumped in the car and drove off.

Laura was waiting in Grandma's room just where we had left her. As soon as we sat down, she asked us if we knew a man by the name of Sam Foster. Mama and I exchanged blank expressions, but then Mama remembered. "Yes," she told her, "I know a man by the name of Sam Foster, but only slightly. Why did you bring us back here to ask such a foolish question?"

A Grain of Mustard

Laura answered with absolute certainty. "Sam Foster is the man who will give you the three thousand dollars you need to finance your song."

This was a preposterous idea. Sam Foster had been in Elkins only a short time. He had moved from the southern part of West Virginia to establish an automobile dealership. We saw him occasionally in the restaurant, but it was merely a nodding acquaintance. How could we approach Mr. Foster and hope to get three thousand dollars from him?

Mama and I thanked Laura and drove away in complete dejection. We talked it over on the way back to the restaurant and decided that Laura had to be wrong. We began to think of others we could approach. Days passed and each time we visited Grandma, we were confronted by Laura who persistently asked if we had talked to Sam Foster yet. It was maddening. Finally, in desperation, I suggested to Mama that we go to see Sam Foster, if only to prove to Laura that her prophecies were figments of her imagination. Mama agreed, so we called Mr. Foster and asked him if we could talk with him on Monday, the day our restaurant was closed.

At the appointed time, we arrived at his home, nervous and dreading the worst, but he was extremely gracious and made us feel welcome. We spelled out the facts from beginning to end, and he and his wife listened quietly, without making any comment. Then we played the demonstration record of Mama's two songs, "You Know" and "Baby Sittin'." The Fosters appeared to enjoy them, so we took the bull by the horns and asked them whether they would be willing to advance the three thousand dollars we needed to have the songs recorded by the Ray Charles Singers. The Fosters looked at each other searchingly, then told us they would let us have an answer the next day.

Neither Mama nor I closed an eye that night. We met at the restaurant in the early morning and, over coffee, apologized to each other for having put ourselves in the position of being turned down by Sam Foster. Our discomfort did not last long, however. About mid-morning Sam telephoned. He and Mrs. Foster had decided to lend us a helping hand and he suggested that we meet him at his lawyer's office that afternoon. The lawyer, compelled, I am sure, by his loyalty to his client, told Mr. Foster he was making a grave mistake, that Mama and I were attempting something that was sure to fail, and that, in his opinion, Mr. Foster should reverse his decision to back us.

For a moment my heart stood still, and I'm sure Mama's did, too. Here we were, so close and yet so far.

Mr. Foster paused for a moment as though he were collecting his thoughts, then he raised his head and spoke with a voice that was warm but firm. "Jake," he said, "you're a good lawyer and you've been a good friend to me. I respect your judgment. But in this case I am doing something I feel I absolutely must do, so please say nothing more and let's get on with the papers."

Mama and I were shaken. Not only were we being given an opportunity to carry on the project, but we were establishing our faith in the visions and the voice that had

A Grain of Mustard

visited Mama and Laura. We knew at that moment that we had an unseen friend, that Someone Up There liked us. The first part of the vision had become a reality.

We sent the money to New York, and the agent promised that the Ray Charles Singers would record the two songs. But by the time the second part of the vision came to pass and the songs were published in sheet music, we knew we were in trouble.

We were in trouble in more ways than one, but I know now that everything happened for a reason.

Our dream of a motel in conjunction with the drive-in was shattered when the State Highway Commission made its decision to build a road that would cut right through the property.

Mama had not yet purchased the building that housed the restaurant. She had only a lease with an option to buy, so we were forced out of business with no financial gain.

About this time, my mother had a vision of an angry crocodile. Instinctively she knew this meant trouble. Before the vision passed, however, the crocodile was tied up on his back, showing his white stomach. To Mama, this indicated that the trouble would be settled satisfactorily. The vision, however, created in us a sense of panic about Mama's songs. We knew we had to get to New York to find out what was going on, but, again, we had no money. We were upset not only for ourselves but for the Fosters who had invested in us and Mama's music with good faith. Because we felt it was the fair thing to do, we telephoned Sam Foster and told him that a series of depressing events had convinced us that we were in trouble with regard to my mother's music and that we felt a compulsion to go to New York to find out what was taking place. Sam and Marion Foster offered to pay our expenses.

Upon investigation, we discovered that ownership and copyright of Mama's music was being claimed by three people who had no part whatsoever in its creation. The artists on the record were a group from the Ray Charles Singers but not those who appeared on Como's show. We had been taken, and we were too ignorant to know what recourse we had. We returned to West Virginia disillusioned and desolate.

When we reported to Sam Foster, he took us to his lawyer. This was the same man who had advised him not to invest, and it was a humiliating experience for Mama and me. The lawyer insisted that either my mother or I must have signed a release for the music, assigning the rights to someone else. We had not. After a long discussion we were able to convince this man that we had never signed a document of any kind, and he offered to help us. We left his office with his promise that he would put us in touch with someone in New York who would help us out of our dilemma. Through one of his associates, Milford Gibson—a former FBI agent who was then U.S. Attorney for the Northern District of West Virginia—he was certain he could find us a responsible lawyer in Manhattan.

That night my mother had her third vision. She saw us in New York. Then we were stepping out of an elevator on the fourth floor. We walked down a corridor, turned

A Grain of Mustard

right, and entered an office that had four names on the door. In the office she saw a long table. We were greeted by a man who was of stocky build, with blond hair. He treated us cordially, but explained that he was a very busy man. He seemed reluctant to help us, despite the fact that we had been sent by his friend in West Virginia. However, before the vision faded, the man offered to lend his assistance in retrieving the rights to my mother's music, but he insisted that he could not handle any further legal work for us. Then the vision was gone.

Mama and I later went to New York. We walked into an office building we had never seen before, but we felt that we knew where we were going. We entered the elevator and got off at the fourth floor, turned right, walked down a corridor, turned left, and there was the door with the four names. The name of the man we were to see appeared at the top. By this time our faith in Mama's vision had become stronger.

Now we entered the office and were greeted by a receptionist. We looked around the room, but there was no long table. Was something wrong? Mama and I waited a few moments, and then a secretary invited us into another office. There in the center of the room was the long table Mama had envisioned, and there, being introduced to us, was the stocky gentleman with blond hair, Mr. Blaisdell.

He was, as Mama predicted, extremely gracious, but he told us firmly that he was just too busy to handle our case. And then he was quiet. Mama and I looked at each other and smiled. Mr. Blaisdell moved around the room for a moment or two, then turned around as though someone had tapped him on the shoulder. "I'll tell you what I'll do," he said. "I'll help you to the point of getting your music back, but I can't help you after that." Then he scratched the side of his head and added, "And I'll be darned if I know why I'm doing this."

Mr. Blaisdell didn't know why he was helping us, but Mama and I had a strong suspicion by this time. God works in mysterious ways.

With no great difficulty, Charles Blaisdell confronted the three people who had attempted to assume ownership of my mother's works, and they agreed to sign the releases that were necessary rather than have suits brought against them. The recordings and sheet music were turned over to Mama. With this accomplished, Mr. Blaisdell gave us for future reference the name of Ed Burns, another former FBI agent who was practicing law in New York.

The second part of Mama's vision had come to pass. But what about the green leaves falling from the trees in the orchard, and the land Mama was to acquire? Could that have meant that when we finally settled the business of the music, and a great personality had made the songs into hits, Mama would get the land to build her motel? Again we wondered. Only time could tell.

Back in Elkins, the days passed quickly. I was busy with my family. But during the quiet moments Mama and I would look at each other, both with the same thought. When would the next vision appear, or would there be no more?

A Grain of Mustard

Through these days my mother changed from the happy-go-lucky person I had always known to someone in deep study. I could almost feel her growing stronger. She not only stopped snickering at Grandma and Laura and the predictions they made, but developed the habit of praying with them.

As time passed, Mama had another vision. She saw Perry Como on a large stage. In the center of the stage was a target. Sheet music was flying around the stage, but in the bull's-eye was my mother's song, "You Know." A voice told Mama to send me to New York, but once again we were faced with the problem of having no money.

My mother put her head back and closed her eyes. When she opened them, she told me to get in my car and drive, and when I heard the song, "God Will Take Care of You," I would know who could help me. By this time I knew better than to resist, so I left Grandma's house, stepped into my car, and drove off, not knowing where I was going or why. I drove aimlessly through the streets of Elkins with my head spinning, trying to concentrate on someone who could provide the assistance I needed to get to New York and to Perry Como. But nothing came to me. When I approached the town square, I had to stop for a red light, and for no apparent reason I began to sing "God Will Take Care of You." As if on cue, a man crossed in front of my car with a money bag in his hand. Obviously, he was on his way to make his deposit. I knew Mr. Shelton—he had been my math teacher in high school—but I certainly didn't know him well enough to ask him to participate in this venture. However, before the light turned green, I found myself calling to him out of the car window. He turned back and got in the seat beside me.

I pulled to the curb, turned off the motor, and told him the entire story of my mother's music and the hopes we had for it.

Mr. Shelton listened attentively, all the while clutching his money bag with the day's proceeds from the filling station he owned. When I had finished, he opened the bag and, without further discussion, gave me the money I needed along with his good wishes.

Before I left for New York, my mother had a vision of my going to visit Perry Como. She saw me in front of a large theater. Then she saw me walking down an alley and stopping before two huge doors. When I knocked, a guard came to the door, but refused to let me in. The next thing Mama saw was Perry Como and me in conversation. Following that, she saw me talking to a slightly balding man with glasses. When the vision ended, Mama told me not to worry. She said everything would turn out fine.

A couple of days before I left for New York, we received a reply to the letter we had written to the Sheldon Music Company regarding Mama's music. They invited Mama and me to come to New York, and since I was going to New York anyway, I decided to make that my first stop. Their representative looked over all the music and said they would like to publish "You Know." I told him I was sorry but that was the one song I couldn't give him because it was for Perry Como. He threw his head back and

A Grain of Mustard

laughed. Then he asked me how well I knew Perry Como. I explained that I didn't know him at all, but that I was sure I was going to get to him and that he would sing this song. I asked him who arranged Mr. Como's music, and he told me it was Joe Reisman. "But," he added, "you have as much of a chance to get to Joe Reisman as you do to get to Perry Como." I thanked him and left.

Like all the other strange but wonderful things that have happened, I did find a way to see Joe Reisman briefly by calling RCA. He wasn't optimistic where Perry Como was concerned, but he gave me a couple of telephone numbers to call with the thought that I might be able to talk with Mr. Como. I was exceedingly grateful, but decided to try to see him face to face as Mama had prophesied I would.

This was the year 1959, and Perry was televising his program before an audience at the Ziegfeld Theater. I inquired how to get there and next thing found myself in front of the building. The doors were locked, but a man nearby showed me the way to the alley. It was just as Mama had told me. I went down the alley and came to two heavy doors. I knocked and a uniformed attendant answered. When I told him I would like to talk with Perry Como, he replied that it was utterly impossible. I explained that it was terribly important, and he must have realized that I was sincere. He asked me to wait outside, but I urged him to let me stand just inside the door. Reluctantly he agreed and then went to look for Perry.

After a few minutes he came back and told me Perry wasn't around, but I begged him to look again.

While he was gone, Perry Como came running down the stairs. I stopped him and told him how important it was that I talk with him. With a completely spontaneous show of warmth, he put his hand on my shoulder and explained that he had to go on stage in just a moment, but he asked me to take a seat in the theater and promised to listen to me after the rehearsal. I was beside myself with happiness.

Following the performance, I returned backstage and told Perry Como my story. While we were talking, his music publisher, Mickey Glass, came along. Perry introduced us, but I felt as though I already knew him from my mother's visions. He was slightly balding but without the glasses. Perry gave me a pat on the shoulder, turned to Mickey, and said, "Take care of this lady."

Once again I related the story of Mama and her music. Mickey listened quietly while I told him of our early experience and the difficulties we'd encountered. Then I told him about the song "You Know" and the fact that it was going to be the biggest success Perry Como ever recorded. He smiled at me indulgently, but I believe he had some intuitive feeling that what I told him would come to pass.

I explained to Mickey Glass that the moment wasn't right for Perry Como to expose this song, but that when the time came, I would let him know and that he could

A Grain of Mustard

count on what I said as surely as he could count on the sun coming up in the east.

During that meeting I didn't reveal a word about Mama's visions, but I had the feeling that Mickey Glass realized that a strong force was bringing us together. Since then I have seen him many times, and he is aware that I now have the gift of prophecy and that Perry's moment with Mama's song will come.

chapter 5

I RETURNED to Elkins satisfied that I had done what was expected of me and with a faith stronger than I had ever known before.

I found Mama restless, her mind full of questions. "Why is the Divine Power helping me? Surely it can't be that I'm such a deserving person. I abandoned my child when she needed me most, violated the Commandments, neglected my responsibilities. Why should God select me for success?" There was no way to comfort Mama or to talk with her about it.

Then one day the answer came. We were at Grandma's, and following our prayers, Mama felt a compulsion to put her head back and close her eyes. When she leaned forward, she seemed dazed. She turned to me and said, "Oh, no! Jeanne, you can't imagine what we're supposed to do!"

By this time I was on my feet. "What is it, Mama?"

Mama looked at me, perplexed. "We're to build a church!" she screamed.

I turned cold with that clammy feeling that comes from fear of the unknown. "What kind of church?" I asked.

A Grain of Mustard

My mother put her head back again, and after a few minutes she looked up at me with an expression of peace. "Jeanne," she told me, "it's more than a church—it's a cathedral. It's white, it's fabulous. And the voice I have heard has called it the Cathedral of Prayer, a place where people of all faiths can come to worship. It's a place for people who have need for something more than they have been able to attain through any of their religious beliefs. It's a place for comfort and cure."

I stood there with my mouth open, then looked over at Grandma lying in bed, her eyes closed in sweet repose.

My mother told me the voice had been very clear, and this was its message:

> You all have listened and I have guided you.
> I choose many, but they're too weak.
> I chose you and you to seek.
> This is a must, and must be done, and this
> is why I have done all I have done for you.

What went on in my mother's head following those few moments I cannot say. I can tell you, though, that I was flabbergasted. What did I know about building a church? Or what did my mother know? She had never been religious. I had accepted my husband's religion, and I took my children to Sunday school, but I was certainly not a pillar of the religious community. Frankly, I was frightened.

My mother sat quietly in the rocker for several minutes,

then closed her eyes again. When she had composed herself, she looked at me and said with complete assuredness, "It's going to be built on Beverly Pike, Jeanne, at a place known as the Cappadony farm. Get in the car right now, Jeanne, and drive out Beverly Pike and find out if there is such a place."

I did as I was told, and, to my amazement, I found the place known as the Cappadony farm. Having gone this far, I decided to ask if it was for sale. The elderly lady who greeted me told me that several other people had been asking them to sell, but that her children were reluctant to give up the place. She was a nice old lady, and I stayed and talked with her for a while; then, realizing that there was no hope of accomplishing my purpose, I thanked her and started to leave.

I was halfway to my car when I heard her call to me. Returning to the porch, I listened in quiet disbelief as the lady told me she was sure her children would decide to sell the farm to me. It was they who determined the price, and I discovered later that the price they set was much lower than offers they'd had from others.

As I started away this time, I looked at the barren trees on the property and asked Mrs. Cappadony what kind they were. She told me that this had once been an apple orchard. "But," she went on in complete honesty, "if you're buying the land because you're hoping to have apples sometime, forget it. These trees are dead; they haven't even blossomed in fifteen years."

I thanked her for telling me, but then, remembering

A Grain of Mustard

Mama's first vision, I said to her, "If I'm to get this land, these trees will bloom again." I left the lady in complete bewilderment.

On the way back to Grandma's, I thought a lot about what had taken place over the past four years. Since 1957, we had been involved with my mother's music, and now, in January, 1961, we had been made aware of the purpose. We had been tested for strength, for humility, for faith. Now we were being tested for sacrifice. Whatever money my mother had was hers, and whatever money she would derive from the music would belong to her, too. If she felt that she wanted to go ahead with the Cathedral, despite the fact that it would eat up any personal income, I decided I would stay by her side and continue to help.

From the time that my mother had her first vision, her sister Bess was intrigued, largely because Mama seemed like a most improbable visionary. I think it was fascination more than anything else that brought Bess to the point of belief. Finally one day she asked if she could join us when we went to Grandma's, and, of course, we were delighted. She sat with us while we prayed, and thereafter she continued to come back day after day.

On February 28, 1961, my mother, Aunt Laura, Aunt Bess, Uncle Mike, and I were sitting around my grandmother's bed, praying, when we all heard a loud voice saying, "*It is coming.*" None of us knew what it meant, but my mother said she had a vision of Jesus with his arms outstretched.

A few days later—March 2, to be exact—my mother

was sitting in my living room while I busied myself with the household chores. Suddenly she called to me. When I looked in to see what she wanted, she asked me to sit down to talk.

Annoyed by the interruption, I said, "Not now, Mama, I'm busy. Maybe later we can have a little visit."

My mother looked at me squarely and replied, "Now, Jeanne—later may be too late."

There was a note of urgency in her voice, and I instantly grew concerned. "What's wrong, Mama? Is there something wrong?"

"No, Jeanne," she assured me, "but you know how busy your house gets, and I want to talk to you while it's quiet."

I sat down and faced my mother. She took my hand and looked me straight in the eye.

"Jeanne," she began, "if you were to get all the money that will come from the music and other things, would you put every cent of it into the Cathedral?" This was a question I wasn't expecting, and I wanted to think about it for a moment. Why was my mother asking me such a thing at a time like this? I knew there must be a reason, and I knew she wanted an honest answer. I began to think of my children's futures and my run-down house. Then my mind went to the people who had invested in me in good faith and whom I knew I would pay back someday even if I had to work the rest of my life. I started to mention these debts to Mama, but she wouldn't let me finish the sentence.

"Jeanne," she said, "there can be no conditions. If you

A Grain of Mustard

receive the money, will you give it all to the Cathedral?"

I paused again to reflect. I had to recognize that if it had not been for the visions in the first place, we would never have had a chance for success with the music, and we knew now that the visions were for a reason. So, clear in my own mind that this was the way it had to be, I answered my mother. "Yes, I promise I would give it all to the Cathedral."

I will never forget my mother's smile and her sigh of relief. "You won't have to do that, Jeanne. I was told to test you. Now I am sure that you will give everything you can to the Cathedral. You can pay back the people who have helped you. You can take care of your debts and your children's education, and you can keep enough for modest comfort. But you must give the rest to the Cathedral. If you find yourself with money, Jeanne, you will find yourself without friends."

I listened carefully and respectfully, but I wondered why it was so important to have this discussion in the middle of a busy morning. I rose to leave the room, but Mama gestured me to stay.

"Jeanne," she said. "I have one more thing to tell you. At four-thirty this afternoon you will witness a miracle." I begged her to tell me about it, but she would not say anything more.

To me, a miracle had always meant something wonderful, so, naturally, I looked forward to the event with great anticipation. Obviously, I still had a lot to learn.

Around noon Mama called our lifelong friend, Clarabell Folks, and asked her to join the family for lunch at my house. When Clarabell arrived, all of us—Uncle Mike, Aunt Laura, Aunt Bess, Mama, and I—sat down at the snack bar in the kitchen. While we were eating, Mama mentioned that she'd had a vision the night before. She told us that she had seen a ladder suspended from the sky and a pair of feet going up the ladder. When she looked closely, she'd discovered that the feet were hers. Then she told us that we would all see something totally unexpected on March 12, and that on March 14 we'd be dressing up to go somewhere. At that point she looked at my Aunt Bess and said, "Bess, you wear my clothes." This sounded strange to all of us. The family had been planning a trip to California in April, and Mama, who was always meticulous, had been fussing over her wardrobe so that everything would be perfect. I thought about the custom-made hat I'd bought her to wear on the trip, and reached over to tap Mama playfully. "Mama," I asked, "you don't want Bess to wear your new hat before you wear it, do you?" Mama smiled wistfully and said, "Yes, Jeanne, I want Bess to wear my new hat, too."

At four-thirty that afternoon my mother walked behind the snack bar, placed her hand over her mouth as though she were going to yawn, heaved two great sighs, and fell over backward.

I was panic-stricken. It was a Thursday afternoon, the one time in the week the doctors in Elkins save for recreation. I telephoned for an ambulance and rushed my mother to the emergency ward of Memorial General Hos-

A *Grain of Mustard*

pital. The staff physician there diagnosed her condition as paralysis, the result of a cerebral hemorrhage. He indicated that she couldn't live through the night.

My mother had told me to expect a miracle at four-thirty. I couldn't believe that a "miracle" meant death, so I could only assume that Mama would live. I left the hospital and went to Grandma's to pray. We prayed that God would send us a vision, that we could find some thread of hope for my mother. But no vision appeared. I stopped by my house to see my children and to ask them to take care of one another, because I knew that I had to be by my mother's side.

I lived at the hospital from that moment on, and I witnessed incidents during that time that I can't expect you to believe, unless you believe in miracles.

There was a teen-ager in the ward next to Mama who was in critical condition and scheduled for surgery. One morning she called to me, and when I sat beside her bed, her eyes filled with tears and she poured out the story of a spirit having visited her the night before. She said the spirit told her that if she was to touch my mother, she would not require surgery. She had already related the tale to a nurse and begged that she be taken into my mother's room but the nurse had refused and had told the youngster she'd had a dream.

Since touching my mother seemed to mean a great deal to this young person, I decided to help her, if only to make her happy for a moment. So when Aunt Bess arrived at the hospital, I asked her to act as lookout, and I smuggled the girl into my mother's room. The girl then did as the spirit had told her, and, satisfied that she had accomplished her purpose, she crept back to her bed. When her doctor came to tell her about her surgery and to instruct the nurses to prepare her, the girl pleaded and begged for more X rays. Her doctor insisted that nothing could be gained from additional X rays, but she was adamant, and he finally conceded. The next day the girl was released from the hospital, without surgery. It was indeed a miracle.

It was on this same day that my Aunt Bess received a cryptic message from a voice saying, "*On the fifth day it rolls off.*" The meaning of these words was to be revealed later.

It was interesting to observe the reactions of the doctors and nurses to my mother and to her family. Some of them seemed to feel very comfortable with us, but others appeared frightened, as if they thought we were witches.

My mother, even at forty-eight, had skin as smooth as a baby's back, unwrinkled and unblemished. And although totally paralyzed, with needles in her hands for intravenous feeding and transfusions, and with tubes in her nose and throat, she looked beautiful to me. One afternoon after she had been hospitalized for several days, I walked over to her bed to look at her more closely. To my surprise and, I might add, horror, I noticed a beard on my mother's face. The hair was a quarter of an inch long and as hard and bristly as a man's.

I called to Bess and told her about the beard. As she

A Grain of Mustard

moved to join me at the bedside, she was accusing me of seeing things. "Jeanne," she said, "your mother's skin is beautiful." Then she was leaning over mother and saying she couldn't believe it. The beard was definitely there.

When the nurse, who had been away from the room for a few moments, returned, I told her, in a way that I hoped wouldn't frighten her, what I had observed. Much to my surprise, however, I got no reaction other than annoyance. "Mrs. Gardner," the nurse responded, "your mother has had that beard since she's been here. I bathe her once a day, and I've seen that beard every time I've bathed her." Bess and I were beside ourselves with frustration. We knew that Mama's skin had always been one of her most attractive features, and we knew that she had not had a stubbly beard.

That night, for the first time, I went home to sleep in my bed. When I returned to the hospital in the morning, the day nurse was just coming on duty and I overheard a most fascinating argument. One nurse insisted that my mother had a beard; the other protested that my mother's skin when she had last seen it had been as smooth as silk. To this day we have not been able to explain the transformation.

Mama had a very close friend in Elkins by the name of Ila Lloyd. Ila was well aware of the fact that my mother had visions and that these visions had guided us in our activities since 1957, but she had never been able to share with our family the feeling of closeness with this Power.

One morning Ila Lloyd came to visit my mother. My

Aunt Bess and I were keeping vigil as we had been since the beginning. As Ila sat at the foot of Mama's bed, perhaps praying quietly for my mother's restoration to health, perhaps just mulling over the good and bad times the two of them had shared, she had a telepathic message from my mother. It was so strong that she instinctively drew pencil and paper from her purse and wrote it down. This was the message as we have recorded it in our family journal:

> *As I lay on my hospital bed of white*
> *There is no day and there is no night;*
> *Just light, more light, and cool heaven's breeze*
>
> *I'm proud of you, Jeanne, for you didn't cry.*
> *You knew, child, that I didn't die.*
> *Now go on your way; this great battle is done,*
> *But be back at my bedside when the clock strikes one.*

When Ila read us what she had heard, we hastened to tell the doctors and nurses that my mother was going to respond at one o'clock. They assured us that this was totally impossible, that my mother would never rally again: she was on her way out. Because we were so insistent, they did agree to let members of the family in the room, and at the last moment they themselves asked if they could stand inside and watch with us.

At precisely one o'clock my mother, who had lain paralyzed for five days, began to move. First it was her feet, then her legs, then her body. Everyone in that room

A Grain of Mustard

was rigid with expectation. Finally my mother opened her eyes. She turned her head clockwise, looked around the bed at all the family. She stopped when she got to me, moved her right hand toward me, winked her eye, put her hand to her head, and relapsed into a coma. Two of the nurses began to cry, another ran down the hall screaming, "She responded, she responded, just as they said she would!"

I left the hospital, so exhausted that I thought I couldn't make it back to my house. I did, but I literally fell on the living room sofa, too tired to go to my bed. As I lay there resting, I saw a vision of my mother. She was sad, half crying, and she was waving to me as if to say good-bye. Then I heard a soft voice saying:

"Trust and obey; there is no other way."

I thought I was losing my mind. I couldn't believe what was happening. I found myself talking out loud.

"What is this?" I asked in angry frustration. "Whoever you are, are you trying to tell me that my mother is leaving me?"

Then I heard the voice again, this time saying:

"I'll meet you in the sweet by-and-by."

I put my head back on the pillows, tired, sad, and terribly confused. What did all this mean, and why was it happening to me? Then I remembered the message Bess had received: "On the fifth day it rolls off." This was the fifth day, and my mother's gift had been passed on to me.

I closed my eyes, wondering as I did so if I could get

through another day. After a few moments I had another vision. This time I saw myself ascending the steps of the hospital, but when I reached the top, I saw a face that was not familiar to me in the hospital setting. It was the face of a lady from Elkins whom I had known for a long time, but there was no reason, in my mind, for her to be in the hospital. I asked her what she was doing there, and she told me she had just been admitted for observation. I chatted with her briefly and walked on toward my mother's room. When I arrived at her room, I found a wreath on the door. Then the vision was gone.

I felt a strong compulsion to return to the hospital. I pulled myself together and set out for the hospital about nine o'clock that night. When I got there, I decided to walk the stairs, rather than take the elevator. At the top of the stairs, someone called out to me. I turned and saw the lady I had seen in the vision. I was startled. "What are you doing here, Mrs. Trahern?" I asked. And as the vision had indicated, she replied that she'd come in that day at four o'clock for observation.

In that moment I knew I would never see my mother again. I walked to Mama's room, and the doctor met me to tell me not to go inside. I will never forget Dr. Christie's kindness as he put his arm around my shoulder. Then, together, we stood in that hospital corridor and cried.

My mother died on March 12, 1961, the day she had predicted that the family would suffer a shock, and she was buried on March 14, the day she had said we'd all be

A Grain of Mustard

dressing up to go some place together. Little did we realize at that time that the family get-together would be her funeral.

Late in February, before my mother had envisioned herself going up the ladder, she had seen a beautiful wreath made of lilies of the valley and yards and yards of white satin ribbons. Instead of the flowers encircling the wreath, however, they were arranged at the base like a bouquet, with the ribbons flowing from it. Mama told us about this vision and indicated that she believed that the wreath was for the dedication of the land for the Cathedral.

Following her death, I telephoned our local florist and asked him to prepare a wreath. I was so tired and so unnerved by all that had taken place that I didn't dwell on the details of what I wanted, but I can recall his kindness. He assured me he would prepare something nice and would deliver it to the funeral home.

That night I had a vision of my mother in a long white dress with high collar, long sleeves, and cuffs that extended below her wrists, and I heard a voice say, *"This is the dress that Daisy is to wear."*

The next morning I visited the funeral director and asked him if he had such a dress. He told me he did not. A white dress was, he said, requested only rarely, and he certainly couldn't provide the one that I had described. So determined was I that my mother would wear what I had seen in the vision that I told him I would go into town and either find such a dress or buy the materials to make one. At that point he offered to search again. This time he unearthed a gown that matched in every detail the one I had seen in my vision, and that is the dress in which my mother was buried.

The other events surrounding my mother's funeral are as uncanny as many of the other circumstances in which I have been involved since 1957. For one thing, the arrangement the florist delivered to the funeral home couldn't have been more like my mother's vision than if he had had a picture from which to copy it. Then, when we took her body to the burial ground, a place I had never visited before, I saw that her grave had been dug just below a beautiful statue of Jesus dressed in His long flowing robes. The emotional impact threw me into a state of confusion.

That night I didn't close my eyes. What was I going to do? If my mother had in truth been designated by God to build a Cathedral, why had He taken her? And what was my part in this whole plan? I felt lost, alone, torn between my desire to fulfill my promise to my mother and my even stronger desire to be free of these overpowering visions and voices that seemed to be with me more and more through the days and nights.

While my faith had grown weaker during those dark hours of mourning my mother's passing, Aunt Bess's faith had grown stronger. She prayed constantly with Grandma and the rest of the family, and she had visions that she recorded, sealed in envelopes, and mailed to us via registered mail. These were to be opened at some future date. She told me that the Divine Power had spoken to her about heaven and prayers and faith, about shepherds and rain and rivers, and that she had set it down on paper as she had been told to do. Someday, she said, a voice would tell us that these seals should be opened and that the contents should be read. I listened to Bess, but I couldn't comprehend. I was too bewildered. As I look back now, I realize that God gave Bess the strength He knew I didn't have because of my physical and emotional exhaustion; then, when I was ready, He provided me with the strength I needed to carry on my mother's work.

Several days after my mother was buried, Mrs. Cappadony telephoned me and asked if I was still interested in the farm. I had to tell her, in all fairness, that I hadn't given it much thought, but that I would be in touch with her in the next few days. True to my promise, I went out to see her, and as I drove the car up the driveway, I was reminded of my mother's vision of the green leaves with the misty light pouring through the trees and the voice that had said, "*When the green leaves fall from the trees, the land will be yours.*" Now, somehow, I felt that buying this dead orchard might be the wrong thing to do. I talked to Mrs. Cappadony about it, told her of my mother's vision, and then fell silent. Mrs. Cappadony shook her head and repeated what she had told me on my first visit. "Mrs. Gardner, these trees have been dead for fifteen years, since lightning struck the schoolhouse up the road. We're just about to chop all these dead trees down." So, once again, I walked away, wondering what to do and praying for guidance.

This was March, 1961, certainly not the time of year to look for green leaves in Elkins in any case. On the way back from the Cappadony farm, I thought about how much I had to do both in settling my mother's affairs and making up to my husband and children for the time I had spent with my mother during and prior to her hospitalization. I would concentrate on first things first, I told myself, and felt relief in my decision.

I derived great satisfaction from giving attention to my home. I cleaned every nook and cranny, emptied drawers and closets, dusted and scrubbed floors, even walls. For two weeks I kept busy, trying to get my mind off the haunting memories of my mother's tragic departure and the tremendous loss I felt. Friends and neighbors were very kind. Many dropped in to tell me they had gone to my mother's grave, not once, but several times. There were people in Elkins who'd barely known Daisy Crawford but who visited her grave as they would a sanctuary, looking to her spirit for guidance. They were prompted, I believe, by the unusual incidents that transpired during her last days in the hospital. I was told that before she had departed, the hospital administration had to restrict the number of people who wanted to come to her bedside for possible healing or cure.

On March 21, 1961, about 7 A.M., my Aunt Bess had a vision accompanied by a loud voice that cried, "*It is coming . . . Eternal Life . . . Eternal Life.*" In the vision she

A Grain of Mustard

saw large white flakes falling in great abundance. "Snow?" she asked, and the voice answered, "No, not snow, but manna." She picked up a flake and examined it and found that it was a thin, round porous wafer, the kind received by those who take communion "in remembrance of Him."

Awed by this experience, Aunt Bess raced for her Bible and read Chapter 6 of John where it reminds us that the real bread from Heaven brings life to the world—as when "Jesus said, 'I am the Bread of Life.'"

On Wednesday, March 29, Aunt Bess along with Ila Lloyd, and other members of our family visited my mother's grave at Memorial Gardens. They parked their car near the statue of Jesus, and suddenly from out of nowhere there floated large white flakes. These flakes fell only in front of the statue and came in great abundance. It was a beautiful sight, and they believed that they were witnessing one of God's miracles. They stood close by the statue and felt the dampness of the flakes falling over them. Aunt Bess's son, Merrill, held out his hand and remarked that the flakes were warm. Then he noticed a large fountain of water which had begun to gush into the air near Jesus's feet and, when it reached its peak, to curve into an arch, like a rainbow. A few minutes later the group returned to the car because of the extreme cold that evening. They sat there for a time, watching a fountain where there had been no fountain, and flakes falling like manna from heaven.

When they returned to Elkins, Ila came to tell me the story. I listened in disbelief, and she persuaded me to get in the car with her and drive back to Memorial Gardens. Once there, I saw what she had described to me. It was a revelation.

Again that night I lay sleepless, trying to satisfy myself that all of the incidents of the past several weeks had really happened. I knew they had, but I couldn't understand why. What was the purpose? Of one thing I was certain. If the Divine Power had performed these miracles to strengthen my faith in Him, He had succeeded. My skepticism had fallen by the wayside, and in its place there was humility and awe.

It was during this time that I experienced the beautiful Easter sunrise in the midst of a blinding snowstorm. My faith was strengthened, but I prayed for physical endurance to carry out the plan.

My children were still young. They needed love and attention. I couldn't forsake them or my husband or my home. And I not only lacked funds to buy land for the Cathedral, but I owed many people who had invested in getting Mama's music published. What could I do but vow to do my best and pray for guidance?

chapter 6

How many times I challenged God during the first four months of being without my mother I cannot begin to tell you. My mind was filled with worry and wonder.

My mother left no money. She left unpaid bills, and there was nobody but me to assume them. Her philosophy of life had been to live each day as it came along. She was good to other people and lived up to her last penny.

I remember one time her looking out the window and seeing my Uncle Mikey coming toward the house, his head down and his shoulders bent in a way that showed clearly he had a lot on his mind. "Look at Mikey, Jeanne," she called. "Doesn't he look like a man who could use fifty dollars?" My mother had never forgotten his goodness to her and to me when the going was tough.

Mikey stomped up on the porch and came through the door like a poor, friendless animal looking for a warm place to bed down.

"Mikey," Mama yelled in a teasing kind of way, "how'd you like to have fifty dollars?"

I've never seen such relief on anyone's face. "Do you have it, Daisy? Do you think you can spare it?"

Mama was thrilled with the joy of giving. "Would I be joking about a thing like this?" she asked him. "Of course I have it, and of course you're welcome to it."

For all we knew, it might have been her last fifty dollars, but that was Mama. She had always been like that, and that is how she died.

So, following her death, I found myself with a mountain of debts. There was the car, one she had bought in my name and which she had intended to pay for herself. There were the loans we had taken to get her music copyrighted and published. There were bills for home improvements and additions I had made on the house to accommodate my mother and her family. And I had the responsibility of carrying on with the Cathedral of Prayer.

Could I be blamed for being without faith? Could I be charged with being unworthy of the task ahead of me? You bet I could! I was floundering, sinking in a sea of despair when I should have been looking for a lifeline.

With God's help, I did find that lifeline in spite of myself. He had shown me the miracles to strengthen my faith. Still, I was fighting it like a sick person who, though physically capable of complete recovery, has no desire to live.

My phone rang constantly, and I answered each call with the fear that it was a bill collector. What was I going to do? I was at the end of my rope.

A Grain of Mustard

One day, following a particularly distasteful telephone conversation, I put my hands to my head and cried out loud, "God, why me? What have you done to me? I don't want to go on. I can't go on. There's no place left for me to turn."

I went to my room, threw myself down on the bed, and put my forearm over my eyes, trying to shut out the world and all my worries. I wanted to go to sleep and never waken. I was frightened, depressed beyond belief, and secretly ashamed that I had let myself get into this condition.

As I lay there halfway between consciousness and sleep, I had a vision. I saw an enormous mountain in front of me, and I knew that I had to climb it. As I got close, I was dismayed to see that the mountainside was covered with snakes. I was afraid; my body shook with fear. Yet I knew I had to climb that mountain. I started up the side, reaching out first with one hand, then the other, grabbing a snake behind its head and casting it aside. There was no end to them. When I had climbed about a third of the way, my legs were shaking so badly that I feared I would fall. Maybe I could turn back. I looked behind me—the snakes were still there—then I looked ahead, and there were just as many or more. There seemed to be no hope either way. I decided I would try to go on. More snakes, more trembling, fear, nausea. Finally I came to the three-quarter mark. I was ready to collapse. I was afraid to look back, and yet I had to know what was there. I turned my head and was surprised to find that the snakes behind me had vanished. Should I turn around now and run to the foot of the mountain while I had the chance, or should I go on and face the rest of the snakes so that I could attain my goal? I took a deep breath and decided to try to get to the top. As I took the first step and reached out to get another snake, a huge hand appeared out of nowhere and took me by the arm to guide me, and at the same time, the snakes disappeared.

True, it was only a vision but it gave me courage. I knew that the road had been rough until now, and I had fear of traveling on. Now I knew that God was still with me and that I could make it with His help.

Money was still my most pressing problem. I was robbing Peter to pay Paul. Needing advice and friendship, I called Charles Blaisdell in New York. I told him I was at my wit's end and would lose everything I held dear if I didn't get fifteen hundred dollars.

Charlie said that he needed a little time, but didn't indicate what he had in mind. I found out later that afternoon when a telegram arrived from him, advising me that fifteen hundred dollars had been transferred from his bank to mine.

There were other incidents that helped me strengthen my faith. Some occurred through other people who came to me for comfort.

I can recall one girl who was suffering from a deep depression and with good cause. She had endured one family problem after another. She called me and told me she just had to talk with me.

A *Grain of Mustard*

Before she arrived, I talked with the Voice, and it said:

> Go to the Gardens, and be there by three.
> Go to the Gardens; I'll be there with thee.
> Go to the Gardens, a sight to behold,
> And watch as the statue turns to pure gold.

I called my Aunt Bess and asked her to join the girl and me. On the way out, Bess and I talked to the girl about faith in God and building inner strength through trust in Him.

We arrived at the Gardens about ten minutes before three. There was nothing different. The white statue stood as always, like a guardian of the grounds. But at precisely three o'clock the statue began to lose its starkness and to glow with a blinding golden light. It was another miracle.

The girl reached for my hand, like a child in fear. And I held it firmly in mine, silently reassuring her that I was not afraid. My aunt and I exchanged knowing glances. God was indeed here to help, and He did. The girl had taken her first step toward helping herself through faith and understanding.

I can't begin to relate the number of times I was told to go to the Gardens, frequently at odd hours, in those early days when my faith needed strengthening. On one occasion, I was instructed to be there at two o'clock in the afternoon. The next time it might have been eight o'clock at night or two o'clock in the morning. The daylight hours weren't difficult to manage. But can you imagine telling your husband, who at this point scoffed at the mere mention of the Voice or a vision, that you had to leave the house at 1 A.M. to go to a cemetery? It wasn't easy.

Spider never stopped me from going, but there were some mighty long periods of silence between us in those days. Later I realized that this was still another test, and it was a difficult one. I certainly didn't want to antagonize my husband. If I could have had it my way, he would have had the same desire for understanding as I had, but I never imposed it on him. Nor did I put aside my own ambitions to give way to his disbelief.

One day I remember the Voice said:

> Go to the Gardens, and be there at nine,
> Go to the Gardens, and be there on time.

Tardiness has always been one of my faults, as I'm sure the Voice knew. I raced around trying to get to the Gardens on time, desperately needing reassurance. When I got there, the Voice spoke again:

> Jeanne, watch the statue turn to smoke.

As I watched, the statue seemed to catch on fire and the smoke rolled up and around it. I watched breathless, helpless, totally in awe.

Then the Voice spoke again: "Jeanne," it said huskily, "this is my promise to you. You will fulfill what you have set out to do."

A *Grain of Mustard*

How could anyone not believe after such a miraculous sight? Yet how could I make others understand?

I confided in my aunt and a few close friends. I certainly didn't want the townspeople to think I was crazy. I knew I wasn't, and the people who went to the Gardens with me knew that I was not, for they had witnessed the same miracles as I.

But one whisper in a community of nine thousand people soon becomes a legend. And the word had begun to spread that Jeanne Gardner was doing all sorts of strange things in Memorial Gardens. I wasn't doing anything odd. I was simply obeying the Voice. What I saw in the Gardens was strange, there is no doubt about that—strange but wonderful.

One evening I was at the cemetery with my Aunt Bess and another lady from Elkins who, at that point, was very skeptical about the tales she had heard. We were standing in front of the statue when we heard the rustle of footsteps behind us in the grass. We all turned in unison. There was nobody there, but there were giantlike footprints, freshly made. I have to admit I was frightened, but I said nothing.

Before I fell asleep that night, the Voice called to me. "Jeanne, Peter visited with you at the Gardens tonight." Peter, I thought quietly. Why Peter? If this were to happen today, I would probably think, why not Peter, if it is God's will? For I now know that all of the saints are with us.

chapter 7

ONE night in May, as I sat in the rocking chair in my living room, my mind wandered over some of the things my mother had told me. I recalled her comment that Mahalia Jackson would one day record one of her songs, a hymn Mama had written which she titled, "He Is Beside Me." At the time Mama mentioned it to me, I grinned and said consolingly, "Sure, Mama," but I knew my mother had never met Mahalia Jackson and I knew how difficult it was to get to famous artists. My mother died without achieving her goal, but now I put my head back and closed my eyes, and I heard that distant Voice telling me that Mahalia Jackson would sing my mother's song in Cleveland during October. I couldn't believe it. Once more I was filled with fear of the unknown. What was I to do? How could I accomplish this impossible feat? When the panic passed, I decided to adopt a wait-and-see attitude. I would try to relax but I would look to the Lord for guidance.

Some weeks later, having flown to New York to tie up some loose ends in connection with my mother's music, I was visiting with Mickey Glass, Perry Como's music pub-

A Grain of Mustard

lisher. Through the years following our first meeting, I had contacted him each time I came to New York. I had never revealed to him the fact that my mother and her family had visions, but my parting shot to Mickey was always the same—that Perry Como would record my mother's song, "You Know," and he would have the biggest hit he'd ever had. On each occasion I would tell Mickey that I would let him know when the time was right. Mickey was always kind to me, but he had never said that he was in accord with my desire to have Perry record the song. It was a game we were playing with each other.

On this day I told Mickey Glass that Mahalia Jackson was going to sing one of Mama's hymns in Cleveland in October. He laughed in his good-natured way and asked me if I knew Mahalia Jackson. As he suspected, I did not. He put his hand on my shoulder and said something about my dreaming the impossible dream. "Jeanne, dear, Mahalia Jackson has never recorded a song of mine. I am sure you will not be able to get to her."

I stood firm. I told him I was positive that she would sing the song in October. Mickey paused, then shot me a sly look. "Wait a minute, Jeanne—you're on your honor. Are you sure you don't already know Mahalia?" I swore I did not. "In that case," Mickey said, "I'll make a deal with you. If Mahalia Jackson sings your mother's song as you predict, your every wish is my command." I was happier at that moment than I'd ever been, because I knew I was on the right track.

I went from Mickey Glass's office to the office of Ed Burns, an NBC attorney with whom our lawyer friend, Charles Blaisdell, had put us in touch. Mr. Burns listened to my story about Mahalia Jackson, but didn't believe that she would help me. As if to comfort me, however, he offered to send the music to Mahalia's agent. "No, Ed," I said, "that's not the way it's going to get done. I have to do it myself."

"Jeanne," he pointed out, "you know this is New York, not Elkins, West Virginia. You know how to get things done there; I know how to get things done here. Let me have the music, Jeanne, and I'll send it to Mahalia's music publisher." So to stave off further discussion, I handed him the music, knowing in my heart that his way would get us no place.

The publisher returned it to Ed a short time later, as I'd known he would, stating in his letter of rejection that this was not a song for Mahalia Jackson. The letter Ed Burns wrote me was one of the kindest I had ever received. I knew he was genuinely concerned about this defeat and he didn't want to hurt me. I was less bothered than he. I telephoned him that day to thank him for his efforts in my behalf and to ask one favor. I then told him I needed Mahalia Jackson's telephone number, and he agreed to get it for me.

I was being guided throughout this experience. The Voice told me to call the number, and when I called, the phone was answered by Mahalia Jackson herself. Had I telephoned at another time, I would have been talking to

A *Grain of Mustard*

her secretary and, very likely, would never have gotten through to Miss Jackson.

I explained, in what I now recall was a very awkward manner, that I had a song I wanted her to sing for me. She hesitated for only a brief moment, then said, "All right, Mrs. Gardner, meet me in Dayton, Ohio, on August twenty-eighth, and I'll sing your song." I had known all along that she would agree to do it, yet I couldn't believe my ears. She has told me many times since then that a compelling force she couldn't explain caused her to agree so quickly. I hung up the receiver and started to think. The Voice had said she'd sing the song in Cleveland during October, yet Mahalia had told me to meet her in Dayton in August. What went wrong? I could only wait and see.

I was still somewhat of a novice at the game of prophecy. My mother, I knew, had had uncanny success, and since she'd passed on, my Aunt Bess had been growing in strength. She had bridged the gaps whenever I needed help. As far as my own ability was concerned, the Voice was a distant one, almost like a premonition rather than an actual voice.

Then came July 4, 1961, and all that was changed. I was sitting in the living room watching television with my husband, and I heard the Voice speaking loud and clear. It said, *"Jeanne, get a pencil and write this down."* I sat rigid and looked around. There was no one else in the room but Spider, and he was intently watching television. I tried to forget what I thought I had heard, but the

Voice spoke again, this time with even more authority: "Jeanne, get a pencil and paper and write this down." I jumped up and scurried around the room to do as I was told, then I began writing frantically. Suddenly the sounds from the television were blotted out completely, and I could hear only the Voice. My husband came across the room and shook me.

"Jeanne, what are you doing?" he asked.

I looked up, bewildered. "I don't know myself, Spider. Just leave me alone."

I continued to write. This was the first time I had heard the Voice clearly. It spoke of the Fourth of July. It told me of the terrible fate in store for Jack Kennedy, and that his name would go down in history along with the names of Lincoln and Washington. It told me that our country would again participate in a total war, but not before we were involved in five areas of international conflict. It told me also that we would be descended upon from the north, as if by a swarm of locusts.

I was shaking as I wrote. I couldn't believe my ears, but I was driven to write down what I heard. When I felt that I was losing control, the Voice said, "*I am signing off now this fourth day of July in the year 1961 at ten-fifty-five p.m.*"

I stopped writing. There was no clock in our living room, and I wasn't wearing a watch. I looked over at Spider and asked him for the time. He looked at his watch and said, "It's five minutes until eleven," and I knew then that what I had experienced was real and not a dream.

A *Grain of Mustard*

The next day I heard the Voice again. Once more it spoke of Jack Kennedy and said the news would rock the nation. I began to sob softly. The Voice continued to speak, but in a consoling way. "*Jeanne, child,*" it said gently, "*I know that war and killing is a terrifying thought, but it is necessary. It is all part of a plan.*" I listened, and I was frightened.

I continued to visit my grandmother regularly, but the situation was quite different than it had been earlier in my life. Despite their strong religious convictions and their daily prayers, Grandma, Aunt Laura, and Uncle Mike had lost some of their faith following my mother's death. They were unable to comprehend why God would take a person who had, after years of roaming, finally settled down and embraced religion. They were angry with God, and they were unwilling to accept His will in connection with my mother. Where I had turned to them in years gone by, they were now turning to me for help in strengthening their understanding. So with a heavy heart I visited their house each day, talked with them, and tried to pray with them, hopeful that they would have a return of faith. Later my prayers were answered.

Now, when I told them that I had heard the Voice clearly on July 4 and 5, they were disinterested. They repeated over and over that all the news was depressing. The world was changing. Everything was bad and would continue to be bad. They didn't want to hear about the future.

Aunt Bess and I clung to our faith. We didn't press the

other members of the family. We met at my house or hers and prayed for the visions to guide us.

Sometimes specific questions would be answered. During other sessions, the Voice would speak at great length about the need for faith, would tell us who was getting a divorce in Elkins, why two townspeople weren't getting along, about an Arab uprising or about advances in science that were being withheld. We never knew from one time to the next what we would hear or in what manner it would be told. One day it would be in short, cryptic clues like this:

>Jeanne, listen
>a pencil
>a sign
>a prophecy
>11-2
>Look up and see
>It is coming
>The called events
>A drape
>The time is set

The next time it might be a passage like this:

This message must reach the next leader of your land. He must listen to me if he wants it to stand. He is President, but I am King over all. People must listen to me lest your nation shall fall. I gave you your earth, your freedom so true. All I asked in return was the love of you. But what

A Grain of Mustard

have you done to your God up on high? You have shunned my word; you know that's no lie. You got the good land; many battles you've won, because I was beside you and I sent you my Son.

Even that has not helped, you Gentile and Jew. Will ye listen to me, or must I subdue? I extended you all you could want upon earth and asked you to believe on my Son and accept your rebirth. But what have you done? You've denied even me, listened to atheists, and denied even prayer. And young children won't know what it means to care.

I tell you I am the King; you must look up to me. Let all people know this so that they, too, shall see that I gave you all this and can take it away. You must stand up for God; there is no other way.

Prayers must be said in the schools of your nation. I command it be done, for I make the equation. Let no one take this privilege away. Some child may be saved if he's taught now to pray. There are some who will know not of God, don't you see? They're not taught at home or told about me. Yet every child must attend school, must listen to teachers, must obey the rule. Still they aren't forced to enter a church door, or to learn about God, or to pray anymore.

Now am I asking very much of your land? I gave it to you. Do you want it to stand? This is my order, and you must obey. Get down on your knees and learn how to pray.

America was my freedom land, my beautiful land, and I still love its children, and I want it to stand. But I cannot abide by this worldly strife. I want people to listen if they value life.

There are other nations who on me don't believe. They are jealous of your nation, and they try to deceive. And you say you know better, but I've led you all the way, have entered every battle, have been with you night and day. But when you cast me out, lose your faith in God, I've no choice but to leave you to rot in the sod.

Now, you must heed my warning. Put God first in all you do. Ask that you learn what is right, and I will see you through. Remember I am your God, your Father up on high. I have given you all you have, and I am ever by your side. Given to you May 8, 1965 at 11 a.m. Amen. Amen.

Had it not been the unswerving faith I had achieved, I would not have been able to carry on. I was well aware of the dimensions of the task I had to perform, but I was totally unaware of how I was going to do it.

The Cappodony farm still loomed before me as the place to build the Cathedral. I needed money as a loan for the property, and I had none of my own. I prayed for help, to be guided to the source of that money. There was no answer. I was stymied. Acting on my own judgment, I visited one of our townspeople whom I thought could be of assistance. And he did let me have the fifteen

A Grain of Mustard

hundred dollars I needed. I, in turn, gave him a postdated check, telling him that if he didn't hear from me to the contrary, he could deposit my check on the given date.

I used the money for its intended purpose and planned my own funds so that I would be able to return his loan on the designated date. My plan backfired, however. I needed money for other reasons and wrote checks in the interim, so that when the due date arrived, I didn't have enough money in the bank to cover the outstanding fifteen hundred dollars. I telephoned the man to whom I'd given the check. Since I hadn't been in touch with him, he was under the impression that everything was fine, and he had deposited the check. I was frantic. My reputation was at stake, and I was praying desperately for help.

I jumped into my car and began to drive aimlessly around town. Where should I go, whom could I turn to? Without knowing why or how, I found myself pulling into the Fosters' driveway. Sam and Marion Foster had already helped so many times before—could it be possible that they would agree to help again?

I rang their bell, and in a few moments I was telling my tale of woe. I explained that I had only fifteen or twenty minutes to keep my appointment to pay off the fifteen hundred dollars. Sam asked if there might be some other person to whom I could turn. I could understand his situation. He didn't have the money, but he wanted to help.

Somewhere in the back of my mind I remembered two distant relatives who were expecting a small inheritance.

They had said that when they got the money, they would let me have it for my purposes, but they had not yet received it. I mentioned this to Sam. He called them on the telephone and they agreed to pay Sam back if he could find it in his heart to help me now.

Without hesitation, he went to the bank and borrowed the money for me so that I could meet my obligation.

This was just one incident of many that followed the same pattern. I had to borrow money from one person to pay another back. It was more than a test for me; it was a test for all the people who were involved with lending me these funds.

I forgot the meaning of pride in my efforts to hold onto the property for the Cathedral. My humility was challenged every day, but I can say with great certainty that the people who have helped me will never be forgotten. Some already have told me that the gratification of giving to such a worthy purpose is compensation enough.

When I drove out to the Cappadony farm to secure the option, I witnessed another miracle. As I came along the highway in front of the farm, I saw the orchard in full bloom. Green leaves filled the trees, and the limbs were heavy with velvety pink-and-white blossoms. Mrs. Cappadony greeted me with a look of wonder.

"Jeanne," she gushed, "remember you said that if this land would be yours, for me not to be surprised if the orchard bloomed again?"

I nodded my head in agreement.

"And, Jeanne," she went on, "do you remember that

you said when the green leaves left the trees, the land would be yours?"

I smiled and told her I remembered very well.

"At that time, Jeanne, I felt sorry for you, because the orchard was totally dead. It hadn't bloomed in fifteen years. I knew having this land meant something to you, but I thought you were in for a terrible disappointment."

"Disappointment, Mrs. Cappadony? I knew I wouldn't be disappointed, but I thought you would be surprised, and you are."

Mrs. Cappadony kept saying over and over, "This is a miracle, this is a miracle," as though she were trying to convince herself. By this time I believed in miracles, and I was absolutely delighted with this one, as I had been with the rainbow on Easter morning.

I drove home that day recalling my mother's first vision of the Cathedral and the vision I had seen since that time which matched what my mother had told me identically.

The building we saw had a dome which represented the world. The dome was gold and white, and it sparkled in the sun.

Fifty pillars supported this enormous dome, representing our fifty United States. There were five entrances, with two double doors, signifying seven continents going into five. The dome rested on five points as a reminder that the entire world would have to rest on the Star of Hope. There were seven sloping stairs to make us aware that seven was the number in God's completed plan.

Outside the Cathedral there were three statues. The first

figure held his arms outstretched, and a plaque at the base read, "I am the way, the truth, and the light."

The second figure held one arm straight up, and the other arm in front of him. This statue bore a plaque reading, "I am the light of the world, and ye are the salt of the earth."

The third figure appeared seated, with an open Bible before him and with two small children kneeling beside him. The plaque attached to this statue read, "Suffer little children to come unto me."

The Cathedral itself was white and the structure was sixty-two feet high and 186 feet deep. Inside was a stage 160 feet in diameter. The area where the congregation would sit was carpeted in red and lined with gold-covered seats. On the aisles we had seen bowers of palms. There were five chairs on the stage with extremely high backs that were covered in fabrics that matched the carpets and the curtains. The red curtains of the stage were hung so that when they parted they appeared as a garland across the stage, in a scalloped pattern.

Between the aisles was an eighteen-foot corridor, and overhead there were candelabra set in the ceiling like a sky of bright stars.

Outside, the orchard was to remain and to be enclosed by a white picket fence.

We were told that water would spring forth from a certain area of the yard. I can only assume it will be a fountain. I do not know the details. I do know that forty trees are to remain outside the Cathedral.

A Grain of Mustard

In my vision I could remember walking down the aisle of that beautiful Cathedral and seeing an enormous crucifix. I cried out, "Lord, what am I doing in a Catholic church?" Before the Voice spoke to me again, I saw a plain gold cross. Then the Voice said, "Jeanne, child, didn't I tell you this was to be a Cathedral for all faiths—for Catholics, for Jews, for Protestants? It is to be a sanctuary for the weary, the sick, the depressed . . . a haven for people who believe in love and who are seeking it, who are looking for peace of mind. They will all come, Jeanne, and they will find their answers in the Cathedral of Prayer."

This last recollection inspired me anew, and I was once again ready to tackle the next problem in achieving my goal.

What is true of most small towns is true of Elkins. News travels faster than light, and as it travels, it is embellished, edited, and distorted. Certain people were delighted that I had secured an option on the Cappadony farm and that I was going to continue my efforts to build a Cathedral. Others were filled with envy and scorn. Some talked about me as though I were a scarlet woman for having borrowed money from men. They knew nothing of the details, nothing of the force that prompted me to pursue my goal, nothing of the humiliation to which I was subjected; still, they talked. Others labeled me insane, fanatic, egotistical, and incurably bullheaded. Of course, I cared what the townspeople said, I wanted them all on my side. But, upon reflection, I realized that most people don't want their names attached to a cause until it is acclaimed by a majority; they would rather brand it unworthy than to lay blame on themselves for their lack of understanding. I suffered a great deal of heartache during those days, but my determination was greater than ever. I had God on my side, and I knew He would guide me through the dark hours.

My faith was my salvation. Without it, I would have been lost. In the days that followed, I was overwhelmed with visions, and most of the time they were accompanied by the Voice with whom I had learned to talk as I would with a friend.

I knew that the Cathedral was only the beginning. I was told I would have to secure more property—beyond a meadow known as the Arch Lytle land—and that one day beside the Cathedral, there would be a refuge and dining room for visitors. I heard the Voice talk of the Cathedral's recording studio and printing house. All of this was too much for me to comprehend. I was told that only faith and determination could bring about the erection of the Cathedral and that I had to take one step at a time, but when I had accomplished my mission, I would have the background to teach other people the meaning of faith. This privilege I would cherish more than anything in the world.

chapter 8

DURING the first year after my mother's death, while I was learning to accept the gift that I had inherited, I was tested over and over again. I heard the Voice at odd hours and witnessed miracles in which I would never have believed if I had not seen them with my own eyes. Often I found myself taking different people with me to observe these wondrous things. At the time, I wasn't aware that there was a reason for companionship, but I know now that it was God's way of protecting my future and of strengthening the faith of these friends in Him and in me.

More and more there were people around me, and more and more there were new faces. Some of these friends wanted to accompany me when the time came for me to meet Mahalia Jackson in Dayton, Ohio. I was still somewhat baffled by the fact that the Voice had told me Miss Jackson would sing my mother's song in Cleveland on October 1 and that Miss Jackson had set the time and place as August in Dayton. Still, I didn't want to fight it. If there was an opportunity for the world to hear the song, that was all I wanted.

At the appointed time several of us piled into a car and set out for Dayton. The trip took longer than we had anticipated, and when it appeared that we weren't going to make it on time, I looked for a telephone to call Mahalia Jackson. I dug into my purse so that I'd have change ready as soon as we came to a roadside booth. Finally, after what seemed like an endless amount of time, someone saw a booth in the distance. We pulled up, I leaped from the car and darted toward the enclosure, only to find that someone had removed the phone. I looked at my watch and realized with sinking heart that we were going to miss Mahalia Jackson's performance and that I was going to miss the opportunity to do what I had been asked with my mother's song.

When we arrived in Dayton, I telephoned Miss Jackson at her hotel. She invited me to visit her the following morning, and during our meeting my faith in the Voice was once more strengthened. Miss Jackson told me not to despair. She asked me if I could come to Cleveland on October 1 at which time she would sing the song. God had never failed me, and I was foolish to have doubted Him on this occasion. While we chatted, Mahalia asked me if I owned a tape recorder. I told her I did, and she suggested that I bring it to Cleveland so that I would be able to have a lasting memento of the first time my mother's music was sung in public.

As we have all heard so many times, "God works in mysterious ways." My taking the tape recorder with me had more meaning than would appear on the surface. Although

A Grain of Mustard

it is true that hearing Mahalia Jackson sing "He Is Beside Me" was the greatest thrill of my life, and that having the tape of it to play at home was a personal joy, it was not the real achievement. When I returned to Elkins, I called Mickey Glass at the Perry Como offices. After we exchanged the usual social amenities, Mickey asked me what was new. I told him to just sit quietly and listen, whereupon I played the tape. When the song was finished, Mickey was quick to speak.

"Jeanne," he began in utter amazement, "that was Mahalia Jackson. How did you do it?"

I laughed at his confusion. "Never mind how I did it, Mickey. The important thing is that I did it, and I hope you remember our bargain."

Mickey remembered. "Jeanne," he repeated, "your slightest wish is my command." So it was that Mickey agreed to try to get Perry Como to record "You Know," and so it was that God led me to this happy goal through His mysterious ways.

With each step there has been a lesson. I have learned that nothing worthwhile is easily won. There are always anxious moments, and only indestructible faith can bring about ultimate accomplishment. With God's help, I had enough faith to get these songs recorded. Now, with Perry Como's faith in God, he will be repaid for helping me by having a hit recording.

One of the interesting sidelights of this particular song is its true meaning. These are the words:

I found you and you found me
Somehow our love is not a mystery
Oh, how I need you, darling
You must know
Say you'll be mine, dear
I love you so
You know how I feel about you, dear
You know how I feel about you
There's no comparing
We'll keep on sharing
*The love that's here in my heart for **you***
You know how I feel about you, dear
You know how I feel about you
There'll be no sorrow
Just a bright tomorrow
With sunshine for our happiness
My new love is calling
My old love said "good-bye"
My new love's filled with gladness
My old love made me cry
*You know how I feel about you, **dear***
You know how I feel about you
There'll be fun and laughter
For you and me hereafter
And we'll love until eternity
We'll love until eternity

It sounds like a love song, doesn't it? While I never questioned my mother about the lyrics, it had been my opinion that Mama had written this song as an emotional

A Grain of Mustard

outlet following the death of an old romance and the beginning of a new one. This was a natural assumption. However, our story does not deal with the natural, but the supernatural. After my mother's death we found among her possessions some notes on the composition of "You Know." She had written the song when she was struck with the realization that she had wasted too many years falling in and out of love, and that her last devotion, her eternal love, was her love of God. Read it again, listen to the music when you can. Then you will understand as I do that this song, like her others, has a purpose.

Through His mysterious ways, I have met many wonderful people whose friendships I treasure, and in each case we have exchanged something good for something good. That, as far as I can tell, is the secret of life. "Give and ye shall receive." "Cast your bread upon the water, and it shall return a thousandfold." These are ancient expressions that most of us have heard many times and have shrugged off as easily as we do "Good morning." Yet, having come in contact with all kinds of people, I have found that wherever I am able to leave something good, good follows. There have been hundreds of instances where I have been met with resistance, skepticism, doubt, fear, annoyance. In these cases, I have walked away with a heavy heart, not for myself, but for those who were unable to see God's hand in my purpose. A little neighbor's child looking up at me with honest eyes, an open face, as I try to explain right from wrong—this is as fulfilling to me as an aged philanthropist who wants to donate to the Cathedral because he feels it is his way of gaining rapport with the Divine Power.

I have digressed from my story simply to make you mindful that this road for me has not been easy, but it has been rewarding in many ways.

From 1961, throughout the next couple of years, the Voice spoke to me of many things, and among these things was the book, the book, the book. My mother had mentioned to me that one day our story would have to be told. I tried to get more information about *"the book,"* but the Voice proffered it in tiny fragments that I couldn't piece together. During March, 1963, the Voice told me to go to New York and once again spoke of *"the book."* This time I heard the name *"Simon Schuster."* I didn't know who Simon Schuster was or how he would play a part in my life, but I took the name along with me when I went to New York.

In Manhattan I was visiting Charles Blaisdell, the attorney who had helped Mama and me during our early plight. I asked him about Simon Schuster and who he was.

Charlie looked at me in disbelief. "Don't you really know, Jeanne? It's not Simon Schuster—it's Simon & Schuster. They're one of the largest book publishers in the world."

I smiled happily. "Oh, that's good, Charlie," I went on. "They're going to publish our story."

Charlie, always the good friend, held up his hand in caution. "Jeanne," he began quietly, "don't count on that.

A Grain of Mustard

First of all, you don't have a word on paper. Book publishers have more offers of literary works than they know what to do with. You're not a professional writer, you don't have an agent representing you. The odds are against it, Jeanne, and I don't want to see you disappointed."

I understood Charlie's concern, and I tried to comfort him.

"Charlie," I said, "I'm as sure that Simon & Schuster will publish this book as I am that the sun will rise tomorrow. I don't know when it will be published, but it will be published, and it will be published by Simon & Schuster."

Charlie bounced back with a fair question: "Who's going to write the book for you, Jeanne, so that Simon & Schuster can publish it?"

"I'm not positive about that, Charlie," I told him frankly, "but I believe that they will write it for me. I'll tell them my story and they will write it."

Charlie laughed at my innocence. "Jeanne," he said good-naturedly, "you know absolutely nothing about business, but even less about publishing."

I ignored that comment, because I knew from experience that it was a waste of time to try to explain my convictions.

"Do you know anyone at Simon & Schuster, Charlie?"

Charlie nodded. "Just by a stroke of luck, Jeanne, one of the partners is a neighbor of mine."

I asked him if he would make a call in my behalf, and he agreed to do so, with some reservation.

I listened as he explained that I would like an appointment, as he answered in embarrassed tones that I did not have a book outline, that I did not have representative chapters, that I did not have an agent, but I fell back in my chair in relief when I heard him confirm an appointment for me with one of the editors there.

I arrived at two o'clock in the afternoon and was ushered into the office of a lady editor, whose face was marked with living and human understanding. So far, so good. She asked me to be comfortable and wanted to know how she could help me. I began by telling her that I had a story to be published and that Simon & Schuster was to publish it. She shook her head and smiled in a way that said, "Oh, another one of these," but she was kind and offered to listen to me. I told the story as briefly and as quickly as I could, leaving out much of the detail, but when I rose to leave, it was dark outside and neither of us could believe that several hours had passed.

I shook hands with Pat Read, thanking her for her time, and as I bade her adieu, my faith surged. I was even more strongly convinced that I was once more on the right track. Pat told me to keep in touch and that she would discuss the project with other editors and the members of the Editorial Board.

I returned to Elkins with a song in my heart. As I had told Charles Blaisdell, I was not certain when the story would be told, but I was sure that it would be told. Of one thing I was certain: the Voice had directed me to the right publisher.

Days, weeks, and months passed and I heard nothing. Then, on my next trip to New York, I visited Pat Read.

A Grain of Mustard

She was again patient and kind, asked me what had been happening in my life, questioned me about some of my predictions and we enjoyed a half hour or more of conversation, but she could offer me no assurance that Simon & Schuster would publish the book. To say I was not somewhat crestfallen would be lying. I felt dejected, but the feeling was momentary. I realized I had to have patience and that God would show me the way. I was still convinced I was in the right place. I left Pat once again, after she invited me to come back whenever I was in New York. I suddenly felt that this was part of the pattern. Wherever I had attained success before, I had had to try again and again and again until the time was right. Believe me, there IS a time and a place for everything.

Back in Elkins, there was lots to do, and while I was ever mindful of my task, I recognized that I had to occupy myself with other things until the moment was right. And I was confident that I would be given direction at that time.

My family required most of my attention, and I threw myself into civic and church work. I had never forgotten the emotions of my childhood, my longing for acceptance, and the surges of exhilaration when someone offered me that acceptance and love. I was one of the lucky kids who had received great benefit from the local YMCA activities. Somewhere in the back of my mind, I made a promise to myself that I would one day do as much for other children. Now that I had the time and the energy, I applied myself to the task and found it most gratifying.

On Sunday I taught a Bible class and finally organized

a group for the tiniest tots who were too small to participate in the regular programs of the church and Sunday school. It, too, brought me a sense of fulfillment and the happy satisfaction of returning in some small way the attention which I had received from strangers as a child.

My husband could not conceal his relief when he saw me settling back into family life. I know it had been difficult for him and for the children during the period that my mother lived with her gift, during her illness, and through the stormy months that followed her death. My restlessness, stemming from my desire to get things done, and quickly, was difficult to overcome. And while I tried to put on a happy face for my loved ones and tried to hide my aching heart and my dedication to my promise to build the Cathedral, it apparently had come through and had caused anxiety for Spider and the youngsters. The children, however, looked upon the Voice with great awe and, in fact, treated me in somewhat the same fashion as I had treated my grandmother when she made her forecasts years before. But Spider was a skeptic who thought of my family's involvement with the Voice as hocus-pocus and regarded my own participation as some sort of foolishness that had rubbed off. This was a situation that I had to cope with in my own way, and I decided that the best thing to do was to say as little as possible. Meanwhile, I waited for the moment when I would have to tackle the project wholeheartedly, regardless of what my darlings felt.

Never through these years has the Voice stopped speaking to me, guiding me, directing me, pointing me toward

A Grain of Mustard

people who needed help. Through Him, I have been able to help physicians in diagnoses, and psychiatrists in their understanding of their patients' minds.

One incident I recall vividly had a somewhat humorous beginning. I had been told by some townspeople that there was a fortune-teller on Highway 33 who, when she had heard of my gift, was somewhat envious. She was determined to meet me, and I, not believing in fortune-telling as such, was equally determined not to meet her. One afternoon a car pulled up in front of my house. I peered out the window and saw a woman, garishly dressed, wearing enormous bold, dark glasses. With her was a young, blond girl. I decided at first glance that the woman was the fortune-teller and that she was bringing the girl with her to take me off the track.

They rang the bell and I invited them inside. My first inclination was to expose the woman immediately, without even offering her a chance to introduce herself. But before I could speak, the girl extended her hand to me, and as I took it an entirely new world opened up. I had been completely wrong. I asked them both to be seated, and I began to speak without realizing what I was saying or why I was saying it. I told the girl about herself, about a deep-rooted problem she'd had that had resulted in a five-year stay in a mental institution. An ugly, recurring dream had broken the balance of this young person's mind. Even she was unable to explain what had driven her over the brink of normalcy. The girl's hand relaxed in mine as I spoke, and when I finished I turned to the older woman and identified her as a psychiatrist from our local hospital, calling her by name. They were both flabbergasted.

Following this visit, we had a little tête-à-tête during which time the psychiatrist told me she had approached me with doubts, but that they had all been erased. She asked about my fee and seemed somewhat surprised that I would not accept money for my help. Had it not been for God's direction, I would be powerless, so, in a sense, I was acting on His behalf, and all He ever asks in return is thanks and respect. The doctor and the patient left happy, with new hope ahead, and my day ended with deep appreciation of what I had accomplished.

This is simply one of hundreds of incidents in which I was involved during the mid-sixties. There were visions of neighbors and townspeople on the brink of disaster whom I hastened to warn, and those with family problems whom I wanted to help, but I knew that I could not spare them the stroke that was their destiny. One day I had a vision of a neighbor who was going on a trip to Philippi, West Virginia. I saw her driving at high speed along the highway, then suddenly her car careened across the road and there was a fatal crash. I telephoned her house and was relieved when she answered.

"Nedra," I began, "you might not like my prying into your business, but are you planning to drive to Philippi?"

I could tell I had taken her by complete surprise. She hesitated for a moment, then answered: "Yes, I'm going tomorrow. But why do you ask?" I told her I'd had a vision and that I was absolutely certain it was not safe for her to

A Grain of Mustard

take this trip. She seemed annoyed by my interference at first, then softened as she spoke.

"I don't believe in prophets, Jeanne, and I can't imagine that you, of all people, could be right. But," she added hesitantly, "I'll postpone my trip."

Before she hung up, I called her name.

"Nedra," I cautioned, "don't drive in your nephew's car, either. It isn't safe."

This was too much for Nedra to accept. She thanked me briefly and rang off.

That afternoon Nedra was approached by her niece who asked her to drive her to a local furniture store. Unmindful or uncaring of my warning, Nedra agreed, and jumped into her car to meet the girl. Fortunately, she had to go through heavily trafficked streets, because, while driving only twenty miles an hour, her steering apparatus failed. She lost control of the car and wound up on the front lawn of a residence. Had she been driving on the highway at fifty or sixty miles an hour, as I had seen her in the vision, she would not be here today.

Nedra was shaken by the incident and swore her niece to secrecy after she told her about my call that morning.

The next day Nedra's nephew telephoned and asked her if she'd like to ride to the outskirts of Elkins with him on an errand. She told him she'd like to go part of the way to take care of something herself, because her car was in the shop and she had no transportation.

The boy deposited Nedra at her destination, and as he drove off, the transmission dropped out of his car, leaving both Nedra and him with no way of getting back to Elkins except to hitch a ride.

This second incident about which I had warned her convinced Nedra. It was after that that she called me and apologized for her lack of belief. Today she is one of my closest friends, and we often laugh about what might have been had it not been for my vision and the phone call.

chapter 9

DURING May, 1963, I had a vision of myself in a gold dress, an olive-green hat, and a fur scarf. I was entering the White House. Even with my strong faith, this seemed preposterous. What would I, Jeanne Gardner, be doing at the White House? I tried to forget what I had seen, telling myself it was a daydream rather than a vision.

About a month later I was on my way into the bank when I was sidetracked by a lady who worked in a dress shop next door.

"Jeanne," she called, "wait a minute." I stopped, and after we had exchanged greetings, she said, "Jeanne, I want you to come look at a gold dress I just got in. It's a perfect dress for you."

I told her politely that gold just wasn't my color and that I made most of my clothes because those that I bought in a store always needed extensive alterations. Then I went on about my business.

When I came out of the bank, she was waiting for me. "Please come look at this dress, Jeanne—I know you're going to fall in love with it."

Just because I didn't want to hurt her, I followed her into her shop. Then, to get myself off the hook, I said to her, "I'll tell you what, Tina, if the dress fits me perfectly with no need for alterations, I'll take it." I felt very safe, because I'd never bought a dress that didn't require more remaking than it was worth.

Tina brought the dress out, and it looked strangely familiar to me. I liked it, and I told her so. Then I tried it on, only to find that it fit as if it were custom-made. Good to my word, I bought it.

Driving home, I began to kick myself for having no sales resistance. I didn't need a dress like this one; I had no place to wear it. Then, as I hung it away in the closet, I was reminded of the vision of me in the gold dress, the green hat, and fur scarf going to the White House. But again I tried to shrug it off.

About two weeks later I was in Montgomery Ward's with my aunt. As we passed through the hat department, both of us spotted, at the same instant, a beautiful olive-green feathered hat. It was on a model perched high above the counter. My aunt clutched my arm excitedly.

"Jeanne," she asked shrilly, "is that the hat you saw in your vision?"

I laughed. "I think it is, Aunt Bess."

Bess called a salesgirl and asked her if we could take a closer look.

The salesgirl looked up at the hat and back at us. "That hat isn't for sale," she told us. "We brought that in from

A Grain of Mustard

outside simply to point up the costume the model is wearing."

Now I really wanted it.

"Do you think the manager would make an exception and let me have that hat?" I asked.

The girl turned away to find the manager, and came back a few minutes later to tell me I could have it.

Bess and I chattered like magpies on the way home, gleeful over the fact that two parts of the vision had become a reality. But what next?

In October I had a call from Mahalia Jackson. She invited me to hear her sing in Washington, D. C., and I was elated. She was singing at Constitution Hall early in November.

When the time came, I packed my gold dress and olive hat, confident that this trip would take me to the White House.

I had spoken briefly to Jack Kennedy when he was still a Senator and came to Charleston for a political get-together. I had told him then that the Russians were smuggling arms into Cuba and that October 19 would mark a week to remember. He listened politely, never indicating whether he thought I was a crackpot or a prophet. And, although the Cuban situation became public knowledge some time later, I couldn't believe that Jack Kennedy, now the President of the United States, would remember me or the incident.

One thing I felt strongly: I should call the President.

And I did, using a number he had given me when he was in Charleston. When the call was put through to his office, I explained who I was and, in moments, the President was on the phone. He asked me to come to the White House about five o'clock and to plan to eat with him.

Later as we sat together, chatting and nibbling on our chicken, I was struck with the terrible realization that he was going to be killed. A part of me wanted to warn him, but an even stronger part of me refused to speak. About six o'clock he excused himself to take a phone call, and he returned to tell me that the Russians had stopped a troop convoy in Germany and that he had to consult with some of his advisers.

That day, November 5, 1963, was the last time I spoke to President Kennedy. However, the next morning, after turning over my terrible thoughts about his impending assassination, I went to the office of Robert Kennedy. It seemed to me that Bobby might be able to help protect his brother. I knew that the President would be killed in a motorcade, but I couldn't determine where.

I was greeted in Bob Kennedy's office by his secretary, Angela Novello, and I told her what I knew. I asked whether I could see Robert Kennedy. Miss Novello suggested that I talk with Richard Kidwell, his aide at the Justice Department, and she made an appointment for me.

Mr. Kidwell was gracious and sat quietly as I told him that our President would be assassinated while in a motorcade. I told him I had heard the name Oswald, but that the only Oswald whom I had ever heard of was Oswald the Bunny, one of the Disney creatures, and this didn't seem to fit the rest of the pieces.

When I finished, Mr. Kidwell thanked me for coming, and I can remember his parting shot: "Who would want to kill Jack Kennedy?"

The rest is history. I had done what I believed was right, but our Divine Power overruled. As He has reminded me so many times when I have questioned shooting, killing, and rioting, "*It's all part of a plan, Jeanne.*"

Typical of a message I have received many times is this one which I have taken from my journals dated July 12, 1966:

Jeanne, my child, I know it has been hard to do.
But dry your tears and don't be blue.
I hear your prayers as you assemble
there in the room.
But the world is now headed for sad, sad gloom
That is about to spread over your land.
You see, it's time now to take My stand.
Oh, they will fret and they will cry and,
Yes, even pray; then they'll ask Me why
I have permitted such a thing to happen to the earth.
It's something that the wretched will have to accept,
And then there will be rebirth.
I shall turn from them and cause tribulation to set in
To show people truth and the wages of sin.
I know you wonder what will happen to those who believe,

Who have tried to be good and My Son have received.
I'll take care of them, child, and all of you, too.
I'll drop a cloud to protect you from here in the blue.
Remember Lot and his story, remember it well.
Remember I saved him, he never fell.
Amen. Amen.

There have been many such messages, with, of course, some variations stemming from particular questions I have asked. I know it is difficult for the average reader to accept and that I might be chalked up as a strange person overcome with spiritual hallucinations, but this is not true.

Several years ago a local doctor who was aware of my gift asked me if I would subject myself to questioning by a team of doctors at a state institution. While I didn't relish the thought of being a human guinea pig, I felt that it was something I should do, and I agreed. After they had run their own tests, they asked me if I could report to a psychology professor for further testing. Again I agreed. At the conclusion of these studies I was told that my spiritual powers did not fall into a particular category of ESP or any of the well-known psychic sciences. These men simply confirmed what I already knew, but I am passing it along to you so that it may open your mind to the fact that there are some people who can communicate with the Divine Power in a way that cannot be explained. As I have been told by the Voice, He does not seek His people because of their educations, their professions, their abilities. He seeks them because of their hearts. If you really open

A Grain of Mustard

your heart, you will find a whole new world of understanding and peace.

But to get back to my story, which now involves my aged grandmother. Through the years following my mother's death, I grew closer to Grandma than I had ever been, and this provided me with the opportunity to repay her, in part, for the kindness and love she had given me as a child. I visited and prayed with her daily. We discussed our visions and prophecies and talked about faith and hope. It broke my heart to see my beloved grandmother slowly slipping away, even though her debilitation was purely physical. Mentally, she was alert and interested, and she looked forward to each day as a child looks to Christmas.

It was in January, 1965, that I had a vision of myself going on a trip, and when I returned, I knew I would discover that Grandma would be taken from me. I was well aware by this time that I had to accept a fatalistic attitude, that I could not change God's will. So I waited.

In March I took a trip to New York, and the vision preyed on my mind so heavily that when I returned to Elkins, I hastened to my grandmother's house even before going home. As soon as I saw the ambulance outside, I knew that the time had come.

Grandma was taken to the hospital and remained there for a month before she died. That month was filled with events as strange as those that had taken place before my mother's death.

Grandma had alternating periods of lucidity and incommunicability. When she was alert, she would speak in riddles that convinced many at the hospital and even some members of our family that she was out of her head. It was I who defended her sanity, because her statements came in much the same way that the Voice spoke to me.

Uncle Mikey and I took turns at her bedside, praying for her and with her.

There was one idea that she repeated constantly. "Lord," she pleaded, "please put my house in order." To some, that might seem to indicate that she wanted to tidy up her home. To Mikey and me, it was obvious that she wanted all her children beside her. This seemed like too much to expect, because, as it happens in too many families, there were a couple of sons who had strayed from the fold. She wanted them with her once more, at least for a moment of understanding.

On April 11, I received a message from the Voice:

I'm calling Sarah [Grandma].
Do you hear what I say?
Believe me, Jeanne,
It's not long till that day.
As the moon rides along, so high in the sky,
Your Grandma will join Me in the sweet by-and-by.
I'll come down and take her; then we'll walk together.
Yes, Jeanne, your grandma and I will be walking together
Upon Holy Sand.
Yes, I'm coming for Sarah;

A Grain of Mustard

It will be very soon.
She will be joining Me before another moon.
She loves you all, My children.
She is a saint and dear to Me.
She has many treasures in My mansion fair;
I've already told her this; now to you I declare
That Sarah's going to join Me.
She'll leap and sing like a lark [Grandma was crippled, remember],
For I love you, Sarah,
And on My ship you will embark.
In getting herself ready
For her Glory Train ride,
She told Me all the truth
And in Me she will abide.
She came to Me many moons ago.
Her face is oh, so sweet.
Her age, she will not show it,
'Twill be a wondrous feat.
For her candle is lit.
Now, dressed in her robe
So dainty and blue,
You must part with your Grandma
For I need her, too.
Now I'm telling you, child,
Believe what I say;
I'm coming for Sarah;
It's not long till that day.

        Amen. Amen.

That is how I was prepared for Grandma's passing and knew that she would be taken from me before another moon.

Not long after that, I was sitting with Grandma in her hospital room when I received a telepathic message from her:

> *Hallelujah, I'm bound for Glory,*
> *Just beyond that shining sea*
> *I have seen the face of Jesus;*
> *He has gently set me free.*
> *Just beyond this world is Glory.*
> *I have seen Him in the clouds;*
> *I shall face Him in the sunset*
> *And dwell in His abode.*
> *I have crossed the sea so shiny*
> *Where He's anchored His golden ship;*
> *He's waiting at the sea of Heaven*
> *To take me on my long-sought trip.*
> *I will dwell in the Holy City;*
> *In Holy Jerusalem it's been built.*
> *I'm waiting with the others*
> *Until the number has been filled.*
> *Peter holds the keys to Heaven;*
> *He is standing at the gate;*
> *I am biding time, my children,*
> *To meet Jesus on that date.*
> *He has sealed me with His children:*
> *I shall never walk alone,*
> *For my Master walks beside me*
> *To lead me to His heavenly throne.*

A Grain of Mustard

> *There's a mountain up in Heaven,*
> *Many saints are waiting there.*
> *They are marching by the dozens*
> *Waiting for the trumpet's blare.*
> *Look for the word in the Bible,*
> *It is written in black and white; but,*
> *It is red when told by Jesus.*
> *Keep it ever in your sight.*

To those of us who loved Grandma and who understood her, this was a confirmation of the message I had received from the Voice. Grandma knew she was leaving us, and she was prepared to go. Still, each day she prayed, "Dear Lord, please put my house in order."

On April 12, 1965, I was visiting this darling old lady, along with other members of my family. Suddenly she began to speak.

"I have to get ready to go now," she stated.

"Where are you going, Grandma?" I asked with childlike interest.

Putting my question aside, Grandma went on. "He got me a cake."

"Who got you a cake?"

Grandma answered me patiently. "My husband has a cake for me, and I have to go help him eat it."

"What kind of a cake is it, Grandma?" I questioned with the same good humor.

"It's a long flat cake, and it's pretty, Jeanne. But you can't have any now, child. My husband has it for me, where I'm going."

There was one person in the room who couldn't contain herself. "The old lady's out of her head," she insisted. I knew better.

That evening when I went home, I asked the Voice when Grandma would be taken, and it answered, *"Two by two at eight."* Grandma died at eight o'clock on April 22. Her birthday was April 28, so that cake she had described was her birthday cake, and the reason she told me I could have none was because she knew where she was going to have it.

She was buried in the dainty blue gown described by the Voice, and before she left us, her sons returned. At last "her house was in order."

Mikey, Hazel, and their family stayed on in the yellow house, but with Grandma gone, it didn't seem the same to me. I hasten to add that Grandma's spirit, which was the strongest I have ever known, still lives today and I am still close to her through my wonderful memories of her indomitable spiritual strength. But Grandma's yellow house which had been part of my daily existence for so many years, now became a symbol of another day.

chapter 10

BECAUSE I had been told in 1963 that my work on the Cathedral would have to rest for three years, there were now two voids in my life, and I became restless.

There were still a great number of personal worries with which I had to contend: unpaid bills, notes at the bank—the aftermath of the projects into which my mother and I had thrown ourselves; and still, I would not ask my husband to assume these responsibilities.

One morning in August, 1965, I sat at home with a heavy heart, silently praying that I be shown the way to meet an eighteen-hundred-dollar payment that was due. I was in a real dilemma, not knowing which way to turn and absolutely confident that there wasn't a person in Elkins to whom I could go for the money. As I mentioned earlier, it seemed that God, in His mysterious ways, had led me from one person to another. Often I seemed to be simply passing the same amount of money from hand to hand as if to test people for their compassion and generosity, and to test me for my patience and humility. But this time I was at my wit's end.

I was so upset that I forgot to take the phone off the hook during the noon hour as I normally do so that I can enjoy a peaceful luncheon. Most townspeople know that this is my practice and have ceased calling between twelve and one.

It was shortly after noon when I was startled by the telephone's shrill ring. I answered, and an unfamiliar male voice asked, "Mrs. Gardner?"

"Yes," I replied.

"You don't know me," he went on. "My name is Titus Schrock, and I'm calling you from Iowa. I've heard a great deal about you from mutual friends, and I would like to talk with you."

I tried to be as courteous as possible, even though I was under stress.

"Mr. Schrock," I apologized, "please forgive me if I sound preoccupied. But you couldn't have called at a worse time."

"What is it, Mrs. Gardner—anything you can talk about? Is there something I can do to help you?"

My laugh, I am sure, had a hollow ring. "Mr. Schrock, the only way you could help me would be if you were to have the keys to Fort Knox."

He hesitated politely for a moment, cleared his throat as if he were reluctant to broach the subject, then threw himself into the question boldly.

"Do you need money?"

"Do I!" I answered with more steam than I should have. "They'll be at my house to get me if I don't come up with

A Grain of Mustard

eighteen hundred dollars by this afternoon, and I've been sitting here this morning as I have for days, wondering whence will come this 'manna.'"

Mr. Schrock seemed to understand my plight. "Well, Mrs. Gardner, it was indeed a bad time for me to call, and I won't disturb you any further. Perhaps when I visit Elkins, the situation will be better and we can get together for a little chat."

"Perhaps we can," I said by way of appeasement, and we bade each other good-bye, whereupon my heart sank lower than it had been before. Time was slipping away, and with it I felt the slipping of my reputation for paying my debts.

It was about two hours later that a telegram arrived with a money order for eighteen hundred dollars from Mr. Schrock. Oh, how I thanked God! Oh, how I praised His goodness and understanding and thanked Him for not letting me down! I had never felt that God had an unbreakable obligation to me any more than I feel that my husband or my children do. I try to do my best for them, and if they see fit to help me, if they feel that I am worthy of repayment, I am grateful beyond words. In this case, the eleventh hour was upon me, and I was certain that there was no recourse but to go down to my debtor, admit that I was unable to meet my obligation, and to take the consequences. Now I had renewed faith. God had shown me the way once more.

I paid my loan and blessed Mr. Schrock and his loved ones with heartfelt sincerity. I looked forward to the day when I could meet this man and thank him personally, but I knew nothing about him except that he was from Iowa.

Months passed and I didn't hear from him again. Then shortly before Christmas he telephoned. He told me he would be in Akron, Ohio, on the twenty-seventh of December and would remain there until the thirty-first for a business meeting. He added that he would welcome an opportunity to visit with me. I leaped at the suggestion. Mahalia Jackson was singing at the Cathedral of Tomorrow in Akron and had invited me to attend. This occasion coincided beautifully. Here was my chance to shake the hand of this friend and to thank him for his great kindness.

I flew to Akron, my mind filled with gratitude. Mr. Schrock had told me he would meet my flight, but he hadn't described himself. When I debarked from the plane, there was the usual milling throng of anxious friends and relatives. But when I spotted a gray-haired man of average height, whose face was etched with the lines of living, I was sure it was Mr. Schrock and headed straight for him. I was right. We immediately hit it off as though we had known each other for years. He escorted me to my hotel, and before the visit was over, he had extended an invitation to me to visit Mrs. Schrock and him in their home whenever I was near Des Moines, Iowa. I told him I would look forward to it, and I really meant it. It was during this meeting that I became aware of the fact that Titus Schrock was Executive Vice President of the Hawkeye National Life Insurance Company, one of the most profitable, pro-

A Grain of Mustard

gressive insurance companies in the Midwest. To me, he was a humble gentleman, a family man who had found peace with God. I liked him very much.

The strange and interesting sidelight of my visit to Akron was that I would not have gone had it not been for the fact that I was going to hear Mahalia sing. As it turned out, she was taken ill and had to cancel her engagement. So I knew that it was destiny for me to meet Mr. Schrock.

It was several months later, during mid-summer, that I heard from Mahalia Jackson.

"Jeanne," she began, "I'm singing in Chicago in one of the city's largest high school auditoriums in August. Will you come, child? When you are there, I always feel the strongest presence of God and I feel that my performance is so much better. Will you come?"

I was happy to say yes. Mahalia had come to mean a lot to me, not solely because she had recorded my mother's song, but because of her deep-rooted humanitarianism. While I was preparing for the trip, I wrote Mr. Schrock and told him of my plans. He responded, repeating his warm invitation for me to visit with his family and him, and told me he would meet me in Chicago. Gene Kieffer, a close friend of Governor Hughes, would fly us back, in his company's single-engine plane.

Once in Chicago, I attended Mahalia's concert with Mr. Schrock, then spent the night at Mahalia's home after having made an appointment to meet Mr. Schrock and Mr. Kieffer the following day to accompany them to Iowa.

I was somewhat surprised to find that they had flown to Chicago in Mr. Kieffer's plane, and in my secret heart I wondered why a man of this stature wanted to share my quiet company and spiritual aspirations.

Once airborne, Mr. Schrock inquired about my comfort. I assured him I was fine and asked him what the weather would be like while we were aloft. He, in turn, asked Mr. Kieffer, who grinned and replied, "Never better—nothing but blue skies ahead." My face revealed my skepticism, so the two men began to tease me about my fears of flying. I explained that I had no fear; it was just that the Voice had said, "*Rain will hit your windowpane.*" I knew it sounded strange even as I said it, and I was inwardly embarrassed for having brought this into the conversation with two men who hadn't known me long enough to have been aware firsthand of the Voice and the deep-rooted faith I had in what I heard.

We had been up about an hour when, despite the clear skies above, the rain splashed against the windshield. The skies remained clear, and the sun still shone. Then in a few moments we were once again flying through clear weather with only the sunshine and blue skies. Mr. Kieffer shook his head from side to side. "I can't understand it, but I'm beginning to believe that you know what you're talking about. Do you have anything else you want to tell me?"

"Well," I began hesitantly, "I was told to brace myself for a rough ride."

This brought a smile from the pilot. "You might be

A Grain of Mustard

right, but I doubt whether it will be anything to worry about. There is absolutely no turbulence between here and Iowa. Just sit back and enjoy the flight."

The one thing I did not reveal and could not bring myself to think about was the prophecy of the Voice that there would be a collision of two planes in mid-air over Iowa near where Mr. Kieffer lives. So I sat back and continued my conversation with Mr. Schrock, using the quiet periods for praying.

Suddenly the plane dropped sharply, then leveled, then bounced like a wagon on a rough road. This discomfort didn't startle me as much as thinking about the third prophecy. Yet I was afraid to reveal what I had heard for fear that it would startle our pilot. So I "put on a happy face" and hoped for the best.

I can't begin to say how thankful I was when our plane descended at our destination and taxied across the field to a safe and comfortable halt. Walking to the terminal building, I told the men about the third prophecy. They both laughed and agreed that I had used good judgment in not mentioning it to them.

That evening the Schrocks and I were being entertained at dinner at the home of the Kieffers, and I was looking forward to meeting Governor Hughes for the first time. No sooner had I been made comfortable in the living room when Gene Kieffer asked me if I had heard the evening news report. When I stated that I had not, he informed me that two planes had collided in mid-air over Le Mars, Iowa, that afternoon shortly after we had landed. Even I was stunned. And yet, in retrospect, I know that this was but another of the "mysterious ways" in which God was working to establish my reputation with people whose faith in me had not yet been fully established.

Meeting Governor Hughes was one of the highlights of my visit. His handshake spoke of honesty and inner strength, and it took only a few moments of being in his company to know that this man had great heart and spirituality.

Meeting Mrs. Schrock was another experience I shall long remember. In her home I felt welcome and at ease. She impressed me immediately as a down-to-earth person, but with heavenly influences. Her eyes were like mirrors reflecting a beautiful soul.

I returned to Elkins with renewed hope and energy, awaiting the moment when the Voice would instruct me to carry on my work with the Cathedral.

My days were busy as they have been ever since I acquired the Gift . . . many visitors, many phone calls, at all hours of the day and night. These intrusions into the already crowded schedule of the housewife and mother left little time for sleeping.

It was around September, 1965, that I noticed myself growing weaker physically; then one day I scrambled to the living room sofa, too sick to get help.

I lay there praying for the strength to call someone when my youngest child, Barry, darted into the house much earlier than was his custom. "Mom, Mom," he cried, "where are you?"

A Grain of Mustard

"Thank God," I thought, "Barry can call the doctor."

Barry was ten at the time and a habitual dawdler on his way home from school. When I had recuperated to the point where I could think about it, I questioned him as to why he had come home early that day.

He told me he'd been sitting in his classroom when he noticed a face at the window, a man with a beard who, he thought, looked like Jesus. Then a Voice spoke to him and said, "Barry, get home from school as fast as you can; your mother needs you." So it was that my little son came to me in my moment of need. It was then that I understood the gift of Barry's life. It had taken ten years of waiting to understand God's mysterious way.

In the days that followed, I had a series of doctor's visits with no conclusive diagnosis. It could be determined that I had an infection in the liver and the kidney, but the doctor couldn't put his finger on what was causing this situation, nor could he control it.

Finally, in February, 1966, my doctor was able to make a reservation for me at the hospital in Morgantown. There I was put through additional tests and examined by what seemed to me an entire staff of physicians.

Through all of this, I knew that there would still not be a conclusive diagnosis and that I would return to the same hospital again.

This worried me considerably, since several months had passed with no improvement, and my three children—Barry, ten; Pam, fourteen; and Bobby, sixteen—needed me.

By now, I had lived with the Voice long enough to know

that there was nothing I could do to change destiny. I was very much aware of the fact that I was only human and that my time on earth could end abruptly, the same as anyone else's.

After I had been in the hospital more than two weeks, I had a vision of Dr. Johnson, one of the physicians who had been attending me. In my vision he was leaving the hospital and going overseas. I told him this, but added that I would be returning to this same hospital before he departed several months hence and that he would be the first doctor I would see.

He looked at me with a fixed expression and said nothing.

I left University Hospital at the end of the month, improved but not cured.

Returning to Elkins, I reported to Dr. Roberts, my personal physician, who joined me in my exasperation over the fact that my problem had not been resolved.

One day I had a vision of another hospital visit. The date was to be April 9. I knew two things. My room number would be 7409, and there would be a death in that room.

I told Dr. Roberts I was sure I had to go into the hospital April 9. He looked at me with concern. "Jeanne," he began comfortingly, "the hospital is full to overflowing. We have tried to get other cases in but there are no available beds even to take care of the emergencies. To get you in, I would have to reserve a room several weeks ahead. So it follows that I can't get you in during April." I asked him

A Grain of Mustard

to try; I told him I thought it was necessary if we were to get to the bottom of this worrisome situation.

He tried and was told by the hospital's admissions office to have me report on April 8. Dr. Roberts was nonplussed. It wasn't until sometime later that I showed him my journal with the report of the vision.

Once back in University Hospital, I was taken to my room—Room 7409, to be exact. I can't say that I was relieved to find that it was a semiprivate room, but I was somewhat surprised.

I was hanging my clothes in the closet when a familiar figure appeared in the doorway.

"Hi, Dr. Johnson," I called out. "I'll bet you didn't expect to see me back here."

Dr. Johnson put his hand to his mouth and uttered a gasp of astonishment.

Later an associate elicited his story from him. It coincided to the letter with the vision I had had back in February. Dr. Johnson had enlisted for military service, and that is why I had seen him overseas. Although he had not been inducted yet, he had been rotated to another section of the hospital and thought that he would never return to that staff. That is why he believed I was wrong when I told him what I had seen, but he was too polite to contradict me. However, when I called to him through the doorway, it was like an instant flashback for him, and now he wondered even more about my gift.

Without wishing to alarm anyone, I told of the vision

I'd had with regard to my return to the hospital, the room number and the fact that there would be a death in Room 7409. There was immediate concern for my well-being, and that concern remained. A constant stream of nurses, doctors, and attendants moved in and out, asking me, "Are you all right, Mrs. Gardner?", "Will you let us know if there's anything we can do, Mrs. Gardner?", and "Rest as much as you can, Mrs. Gardner."

The following morning, in the early hours, I heard gasping from the other bed. I reached for the cord to call a nurse, but the patient had already pressed her bell. It was too late. In moments she was gone. So it was that another vision had come to pass as a reality.

The word soon got around the hospital that I had prophesied my room number and the fact that there would be a death in that room. I had visitors around the clock: patients, doctors, nurses, kitchen attendants, laundry workers, everyone seeking some word about themselves, their loved ones, or prophecies of national or international significance. I was amused by this interest and aware through all of it that my power would be given only to help someone who needed it.

I returned to Elkins with my own medical problems still unsolved but with hope that a miracle drug would restore me to normal health. Even now I am not completely well, but I am able to get through my day's activities, and for this I am very thankful.

Many times I have asked the Voice why, if He selected

A Grain of Mustard

me to help Him, He impaired my health. And the Voice answered that wherever He has sent me, there has been a need for my presence. *"Question not, Jeanne, my child, it is all part of My plan."*

chapter 11

As I mentioned earlier, my mother's hobby was playing the piano, but she could not read or write music. The Voice gave her a song—both words and music—and she put it down on paper immediately. If she didn't write it down, it would never come to her again. Since she had no training in music, she simply indicated ti-fa-sol-re, and so on, where the notes belonged; then she took the paper to a friend who set it out properly so other people could sing and play it. When the Voice gave her a song, He also told her which artist or artists would someday make it popular.

There were sixty-five songs in all. During the past eight years, I have been able to have all of them copyrighted and have made contacts with many of the people who will record them for the public. In His mysterious way, He has led me to these recording stars so that when the time is right, I will have the groundwork laid. There is a message here that applies to everyone. It is simply this: when you make your plans, set your goals, decide what you want out of life, prepare a mental blueprint. Then cut your paths to take you in the proper direction. I can tell you firsthand

A Grain of Mustard

that patience is one of the most important ingredients in planning. The worthwhile things take time.

I can remember when I heard the Voice repeatedly mentioning *"Baby Sittin',"* *"Eddie Fisher,"* and *"it is a Ramrod."* "What is a Ramrod?" I would ask, and the Voice would answer, *"Use your wisdom, Jeanne."*

I pondered, I went back over my journals for clues, I consulted the dictionary, and I found myself right back where I was in the first place—nowhere. Then one day I was in the office of the attorney, Ed Burns, and I was telling him about the confusing message I had received regarding this song.

Ed looked at me in amazement. "Jeanne," he laughed, "this one is too easy. Eddie Fisher records through his own production company which he calls Ramrod Productions."

I saw what Ed meant. I hadn't been able to see the forest for the trees.

So I called Ramrod Productions, and I was told that Eddie Fisher wasn't in. "Is he in town?" I asked.

"Yes, he's at his hotel," the operator said and rang off.

Once more I called Ed Burns and asked him to find out where Eddie Fisher was staying in New York. Ed gave me the name of the hotel, closing the conversation with one more word of caution: "Don't expect to get him through the switchboard, Jeanne. People like Eddie Fisher have private numbers, and I can't get that number for you."

I thanked him and told him I'd try with the information I had.

Surprisingly, when I called the hotel, they put me

through without hesitation, and the person who answered the phone in Eddie Fisher's suite was Eddie Fisher. I explained that I had a song for him, and he asked me to come over.

I remember clearly my first impression of the elegant hotel and later the feeling of awe as the elevator carried me to his floor and let me out, not in a public hallway, but in the foyer of his apartment. He had a large suite, and the furnishings were sumptuous. For a brief moment I wondered what I was doing there; then I remembered my mission and quickly set about trying to accomplish it.

Eddie Fisher was the answer to a prayer. He was as normal as blueberry pie and put me at ease in seconds.

As luck, or God, would have it, his special arranger was with him. I handed Eddie the sheet music, and he placed it on the piano for the arranger to play. Eddie sang it through a couple of times, smiled his disarming smile, and gave me hope. "I like it. Perhaps someday I can record it."

I smiled back. "You will, Mr. Fisher, you will," I responded knowingly.

The story of "Somebody Cares" was similar. In this case the Voice told us the song would be recorded by Connie Francis. *You will go to New York,* the Voice said to me, *"and meet Connie Francis, but only for one reason."* I bided my time as I had learned to do. Months passed, then one day Mahalia Jackson called me and invited me to hear her sing at Lincoln Center in New York. I jumped at the opportunity. Following the recital there, we went to the Americana Hotel, where Mahalia was staying and I called

A Grain of Mustard

George Franconero, Connie Francis's father. When we met, Mr. Franconero and I hit it off instantly, and I found myself telling him about the songs. I told him that I knew I had a song that would be perfect for his daughter.

Mr. Franconero suggested that I write a letter to Connie's manager, but I had learned from past experiences that the Voice did not want someone else to do my work, that I had to do it myself as I had in the case of Mahalia Jackson.

While I was still in New York, Mahalia took me to the rehearsal for the Ed Sullivan Show, and much to my delight and amazement, Connie Francis was one of his guests. After the show Mahalia introduced me to Connie and that is how I made the contact that will hopefully bring about her recording of "Somebody Cares."

Where these songs are concerned, each one seems tailor-made for the individual who has recorded it or will record it. It is as though the Voice were giving that person a reward for having done something fine for Him.

As I've said before, God judges people by their hearts. I have asked the Voice time and time again why He has selected only certain people to do His work, and the Voice has answered, *"Jeanne, everyone is called, but not everyone responds."* God doesn't judge individuals by their adherence to man-made doctrines. God judges you by your heart, your acknowledgement of your fellow man, the sense of decency with which you conduct yourself in situations that are facing you.

One day I heard the Voice saying, *"By My big window*

you're sitting, Kay Starr." I asked the Voice what that meant, and the Voice answered, "*Use your wisdom, Jeanne.*" This was an expression the Voice used frequently. Every time I heard it, I thought to myself, "What wisdom?" But as the days and weeks and months passed, I was given additional clues until the entire puzzle fell into place:

> *By My big window you're sitting, Kay Starr.*
> *You will meet her;*
> *I will show you the way.*
> *"I Want to Belong to Someone"*

"I Want to Belong to Someone" was another of my mother's songs, and the fact is that if Kay Starr had written it herself, it couldn't have been better suited to her voice and style. It was one of my favorites, and I couldn't have been happier at the prospect of Kay Starr's recording it, but how? When? How was I going to meet her?

Again I waited.

Months passed, and once more I found myself in New York, making the usual rounds to see Charles Blaisdell, Ed Burns, Mickey Glass, and my friend Pat Read at Simon & Schuster, who still gave me no encouragement with regard to publishing my story.

When I called Mickey Glass, he invited me to a Perry Como rehearsal. There, as if by design, I met Kay Starr and had an opportunity to discuss with her the song, "I Want to Belong to Someone," and to tell her about the

A *Grain of Mustard*

Cathedral. She was immediately receptive and suggested that I send her the music when I knew the time was right.

This is the way it has been again and again. I have encountered many people who did not seem to fit into the pattern at the time of our meeting. Yet now I know that God put me in their paths to make them ready for a future purpose.

So has it been with the President of the American Broadcasting Company, Hugh Downs of the *Today Show*, the President of the National Broadcasting Company, and many, many others.

I can recall the time the Voice told me to visit Cyrus Vance concerning the Bond Drive and the escalation of the war. He was then Deputy Secretary of Defense under Mr. McNamara. I asked Richard Kidwell, Robert Kennedy's aide, for his help, and he told me how to make the appointment. The date was set for Saturday morning at the Pentagon. Somehow, in my haste to be on time, I left Mr. Vance's room number and telephone extension back at my hotel, some thirty minutes away by taxi.

Nevertheless, I followed the instructions given me by Cyrus Vance and entered the building by the River Entrance. There I was stopped by a guard who asked to see my pass. I told him I had none, but that I had an appointment to see Cyrus Vance and that the conversation I was having right at that moment was making me late. The guard looked at me, firmly convinced, I am certain, that I had no business being there. He agreed to call Mr. Vance's office, in any case, and an aide was sent down to the desk to usher me in. What relief!

The Voice had given me a number of clues that would be helpful in my initial discussions with Mr. Vance, and they were magical. I liked Cyrus Vance. I liked the way he looked at me in disbelief when I told him things about himself, then threw his head back and laughed, as if my visit were some kind of practical joke. He couldn't understand how I knew these things.

After we talked about Mr. Vance and the future, I told him about a song my mother had written for a Bond Drive that would be staged by our government shortly. She called the song "Our Victory." Mr. Vance suggested that I visit the Bond Division of the Treasury Department and told me whom to see there. I was most grateful.

As I left the Deputy Defense Secretary's office, one of his aides stopped me. Placing his hand cordially on my arm, he said, "I don't know why you came to see Mr. Vance, but I would like to tell you this. I have been his aide for many years, and I have never seen him so relaxed. He is normally a very somber, very serious man with little time for laughter."

I followed the advice given to me by Cyrus Vance and made an appointment at the Bond Division of the Treasury Department where I told Mr. Halbert about "Our Victory." As I recall, I sang it for him, and although I am not a professional singer, he was moved sufficiently to take me to his boss, Edmund Linehan, who is Director of Advertising and Promotion for the Bond Division. I ex-

A Grain of Mustard

plained to Mr. Linehan that Kate Smith was going to sing the song and that I was sure, through this song, the Bond Drive would achieve overwhelming results. He had two questions. Could we change the name and corresponding lyrics to "Our Security," and how did I know it would be Kate Smith?

I couldn't answer him without revealing the entire story of the visions and the Voice, and I wasn't yet ready to go into details like that. So I simply smiled and told him that these were details that I thought time could solve. Hopefully, the Bond Division's enthusiasm will bring the results prophesied by the Voice.

It was about the same time that the Voice directed me to call *"a spokesman for RCA."* So, when I was back in New York, I telephoned the RCA number and asked the switchboard operator for General Sarnoff. When his secretary answered, I asked if I might talk to General Sarnoff. After identifying myself, I spoke with him briefly, and told him a little about the song, "Our Victory." He was extremely pleasant but referred me to a man by the name of Engstrom who suggested that I "drop in sometime" when I was in the neighborhood. Accepting his casual invitation, I stopped by the RCA executive offices one day when I was walking through Rockefeller Center. The lobby directory gave me no clue as to Mr. Engstrom's position with the company. Only his name was listed.

Having reached the executive floor, I approached the receptionist. "Mr. Engstrom," I said confidently.

"Do you have an appointment?" she countered.

"No, I don't," I replied, a little less confident.

The girl was patient, but firm. "Dr. Engstrom," she said with emphasis on "Dr.", "doesn't see people except by appointment."

"He doesn't?" I sputtered. "I was told to just drop in when I was in the neighborhood."

The receptionist seemed somewhat skeptical, but reached for the telephone. "What is your name?" she inquired through half-closed eyes. I told her, and she rang Dr. Engstrom's office. When she hung up, she looked at me and said, "I'm sorry, Mrs. Gardner—Dr. Engstrom would be delighted to see you." I thanked her and had started down the corridor when I heard her call to me. "Do you know your way? Do you know which office is his?"

I admitted I did not. I had planned to find it on my own.

She motioned with her hands. "When you get to the end of this hallway, turn left, walk to the end of that hall, past the Board Room. General Sarnoff's office is on the left, and you'll find the President's office on the right."

"The President's office!" I couldn't believe it. Why was I going to see the President of RCA? What did it all mean?

Smilingly, I wondered what kind of game the Voice was playing with me.

I was still smiling when a secretary introduced me to Dr. Engstrom. "What's so funny?" he asked. I explained that while I knew he was an executive, I had not been

A Grain of Mustard

aware until a moment before that he was President of the company, and that this time was the first time I had been taken to a president's office without knowing why.

Then we talked about "Our Victory" and the Bond Drive. We parted with his promise to help me in any way he could when I was ready. I smiled again, realizing that my readiness depended entirely on the Voice.

It was Dr. Engstrom who arranged for me to meet with Robert Kintner, President of NBC. It was Mr. Kintner who, in turn, steered me to Sidney Eiges, Vice President in charge of Public Information. All of this was for the same ultimate purpose—to pave the way—so that when the time was right, I would have all the connections to tie this enormous program together.

I always headed toward New York with hope in my heart and a prayer that my project was nearing completion, and I always returned to Elkins satisfied that I had performed as the Voice had instructed me, but still with a great deal of anxiety and the ever-constant question, "When will I come to the turning in the road?" But, as I said, with God's work we learn patience.

I had learned to live with God and to trust in Him as I had never trusted before. With this faith, I have been able to see each day through and to wait for His next direction.

The messages from the Voice were spasmodic. Sometimes I would hear Him several times a day. Sometimes weeks would pass and I would hear nothing.

And it always seemed that when I would reach a point of despair, He would come through, either with some little tidbit to entertain me, some local gossip perhaps, or with a beautiful heart-warming message to help me keep my faith. In looking back over my journals, I discovered one such message that I would like to share with you. It is dated September 27, 1965.

Child, the pesticides now strike your land;
It's one, then another, so take your stand.
Tell all about Me, the things I conceive;
Tell all the story, so they will believe.
Oh, some will laugh, and some will jeer;
Pay no attention; right now, they lack fear.
But you may be certain that it won't be long
Till those in doubt sing a different song.
Look at Noah as he built the ark:
People scoffed at him from light until dark,
But he went right on with zeal and vim;
He believed, and his light never grew dim.
But what happened to those who did not believe?
I cast them from Me.
They disappeared into the bottom of the sea.
I have left many messages for you to deliver, Jeanne.
Please continue My work and keep the slate clean.
More will pay attention to the things you will say,
For soon they will know that there's no other way.
Oh, your trials and troubles showed you many locked doors,
But what I'm going to do will give you trouble no more.
You see, I have to wait; we all have to wait for the perfect
    time.

A Grain of Mustard

There's a strong message here, this is not just a rhyme.
I know you've oft thought I was just in your mind;
Then you opened your eyes, and a surprise you did find.
I've told you My promise to you and Daisy I'd keep,
But it has to come slowly, and not in one sweep.
Many will listen who wouldn't before.
Be good to each one, Jeanne; it's part of your chore
That I have asked you to do for Me.
You've always sought God, and God has sought thee.
You know I am the way to all solutions,
That by the touch of My hand, I make all resolutions.
And in your turmoils, as your head goes 'round,
You know in your heart God won't let you down.
Jeanne, I know the faith you've extended to Me;
You've believed in My word, and your faith set you free.
I want you to work with the young of the world:
It may be a boy, it may be a girl.
I have selected many to help with this work,
And those I have chosen, like you, will not shirk.
The Cathedral will have many far points to reach.
Each helper will have work to do, and a chosen few will preach.
But I'll give them the words.
They will speak and preach, my dear,
And will do the tasks I give them, never having fear.
Remember what I said before.
"Where two or more are gatherin'"
I will hover in their midst,

And wipe away the sin.
Each one who will help you will never be alone,
For his God will be beside him, wherever he may roam.
Now, child, do you understand what I've been saying to you?
Remember, I spake and will continue to speak to all from here in the blue.
Some will not listen who come to you, Jeanne,
But treat them with kindness; don't ever be mean.
Just do as I ask you, leave the doubters to Me.
Then someday they'll know that God has spoken truth through thee.
Amen. Amen.

I remember vividly the day I received this lengthy message. My hand hurt from writing so quickly, and when I had finished, I had difficulty deciphering what I had written. So I wrote it again, this time more clearly. Then I read it over and over. In its entirety, the thought was uplifting, but what about the first part? What about "*pesticides striking the land*"? I felt that this line was important to the overall message. The Voice had spoken several times earlier of famine and the need for storing up food. Could it be that the pesticides would ultimately make our farmland inoperable? I made a mental note to ask Him the next time I had contact.

A day or so later the Voice spoke again. The tone was angry, so angry, in fact, that I forgot my question.

A Grain of Mustard

Jeanne, you must tell the people of your land
That I can destroy them by the touch of My hand;
For I'm the Almighty who reigneth on High.
I say who shall live, and I say who shall die.
These poor people have much to learn;
They must seek their true God, or they shall all burn.
The time will come to destroy the old earth,
But some will remain who shall have their rebirth.
I'll judge every one, and many will grieve;
'Twill be too late for help then; they'd better believe.
I let My Son die for the sins of the land;
Now all must repent if they join My band.
I'm depending on you, Jeanne, to carry the word;
Tell all of My Voice and the things you have heard.
I'm Alpha, Omega—the beginning and end.
I'm calling Christian and Jew to me to repent.
For I am the Father, the King up above,
Who looks over all; I speak as the dove.
                                Amen. Amen.

On August 13, 1967, I received one of my longest messages, and I was shaken as I scrawled it on a pad in my bedroom. The Voice was emphatic in tone:

Jeanne, there is much to do. Ye must not slow down. Work, for the night is coming. Work until man's work is done. Work, ye must! Work for the Father and for the Son! Time waits for no man. Watch it well, or it will pass ye by. Ye have a job to do. Hurry. Make haste. There are many to help. This is an alternative for your nation; there must be constitutional amendments. Ya! If this is not done, watch and wait for the outcome. To those who refuse I say, "There is no need of a Senate if there is no nation." Some think naught of this message. To them I say, "Fear had better enter your hearts, for I can do anything. I come in a twinkling of an eye. I give no warnings later; My warnings are now."

Take heed and believe Me, little one. I send ye on a great mission for you are God's helper. Stand up. Show that you believe. I am beside ye to guide ye all the way. Ye have a great job to do for your nation. Again, my child, I say hurry. There is much to do. Later, no reprieve.

I always give people a chance. Ye know this is only groundwork for a higher plane. What ye perform on earth determines the height ye will reach on the next plane, the New World. Did I not tell you many years back that ye shall leave this one and go higher?

Few people ask for my help, ask to be shown their purpose. Those I cannot guide. But you have faith, Jeanne, and you know what ye must do. You have always come to Me, and I have never refused you.

Ye know I am Peace. Ye know I am Love. Ye know I am Contentment. I am all. Remember the words, "God above all." Good words, ya! They mean what they say. Ye must put God above all. Let nothing stand in your way. Earthly treasures mean nothing if ye are not assured a home in the New World. When bodies are laid to rest,

A Grain of Mustard

some shells will be left. Those who have not denied Me shall have new life and shall be lifted to the New World. They shall ascend on a cloud of glory.

Everything in the New World is glorious. No sickness. No pain. No sorrow. No tears. Only many glad tomorrows.

Each will have a job to do in the New World. How important the job is will depend on the good works ye do on the old earth. Earth was put there only for your footstool, to give each a chance to prove his merit for that other home, the home that is really home.

What is it like, ye've been asking, Jeanne. It's glorious, child. No earth-like exchange is needed there. There is no jealousy, no greed. Only love of God and a spirit of fellowship . . . happiness untold . . . a wealth that would be impossible for ye to comprehend. It's too big for you, Jeanne, and for your fellow man. Ya, scientists have thought they knew. They are searching into space; but, I say to you, Jeanne, space was not meant for your people. I let them go, and I will let them go as far as I say they shall go. Watch, child. I have told you they will reach the moon; I have told ye this before. But Peace exists away from all these so-called heavenly bodies. Ye shall not take your greed into space. No hate shall live there. Heed these words well. I speak the truth. I know all. I see all.

Again, I say to you, there is much to be done. Work fast. Ye know well what I have said many times. I choose many to help. Some will; some will not. Those who heed my word, I will move the way I have led ye.

Ye have worked for Me, child. Ye have made sacrifice. But I pay well. What I have asked is small compared to what I shall do for you. Ye have worked hard, Jeanne, and ye will win.

Woe be unto those who will not work. I will remove. I will repay. I will give vengeance.

It is your duty now to show others the way. You have learned to turn the other cheek. Ye have marked My words well. Now continue to do this for Me, little one. Keep your great faith. Ya, keep your confidence. Let not man change your thinking. Remember everything that you have learned these years. I will be with you. I will let you know dates, I will let you know times. I will keep you and those who helped you safe.

Do you listen, Jeanne? It is your duty to warn man that he has not the right to take God's work into his hands. Man is nothing when he is destructive. While he destroys others, he is destroying himself. Only I can help. All must believe. They must heed this warning. Tell the story, Jeanne; help others to find faith.

Tell them that from the tiny acorn comes the mighty oak, but that there would be no acorn were it not for this Mighty Oak.

Tell the story, Jeanne. It must go all over the world. It is a story for everyone, for Protestant, for Catholic, for Jew. It is a story for all, for there is but one religion. All people are My children. Tell them for me, Jeanne. Teach them not to worship idols, not to worship other humans, not to

A Grain of Mustard

worship money or its prizes. Help, Jeanne. Help others to find themselves. All people must have a chance to know I am here.

I can bring riches, I can bring hunger. I can do it in the twinkling of an eye.

Many do not understand. Look to Me and I will give ye knowledge. Ye will become an instrument of My hand, and with My hand ye will know peace and happiness.

Remember, you are doing this for Me, Jeanne. Work. Make haste. The enemies of all people lurk in darkness. I go now, My child. Rest in peace for I love ye. Amen Amen.

What was I to do that I had not done already? The best way I knew to reach the multitudes was to have our story of the gift published in a book. I had been told by the Voice to go to Simon & Schuster, but at this moment Simon & Schuster had given me no encouragement. Was there some other way that I was too blind to see? I had no money to travel and spread this word, and even if I did, who would listen? Where could I go where I would be believed by the masses?

chapter 12

THERE was no other solution that I could see. I had to do it the way the Voice had directed me. I would "turn the other cheek" once again and go to Simon & Schuster. As I said, this was mid-August, 1967. Before the end of that year I was to visit New York City twice and twice leave there dejected. There appeared to be little hope of publishing the story, and I searched frantically for another way to perform my task. My only comfort were the words, "*It must be done, Jeanne. I will show you the way.*"

It was early in 1968 that the Voice spoke once more of "*the story, the story . . . the time is coming . . . I will show you the way.*" Although I wanted to get on with the story, because I knew that this would be a major step in the building of the Cathedral, I was frightened. I had been calling on Pat Read, an editor at Simon & Schuster, through the years since I'd been given the gift of prophecy, but she was unbending in her first response. She told me that unless I could find someone to write the story or an outline and representative chapters Simon & Schuster could not begin to give consideration to the idea. Once more I

A Grain of Mustard

decided to put my faith in God and wait for His guidance.

The tone of the Voice grew stronger each time it would mention the story, until the moment arrived that I knew I had to do something. I went to New York and through people I had already met, I found a man who said he would write the story in capsule form, as an indication of his style, for one thousand dollars. Having no experience in this area, I took his word that this was a reasonable fee. He performed his work speedily, and I paid him, hoping that his presentation would win the hearts of the Editorial Board at Simon & Schuster. With great expectancy, I handed the work over to Pat Read, who told me that I might just as well go back to Elkins and wait for the answer, because the Board wouldn't be meeting for another week.

So once again I returned to Elkins to wait and to pray, and the days passed like endless years.

Finally, in March, the postman handed me a letter from Simon & Schuster, Inc. With trembling hands, I carried it into the house. Much to my surprise and disappointment, the letter was not from Pat Read but from Bea Moore, whom I'd never met. Mrs. Moore, it seemed, was a publisher of one of the other divisions of Simon & Schuster. She told me that Pat Read had spoken to her about me and my story and that the Editorial Board of the hard-cover Trade Division was not inclined to accept it for publication. Pat had therefore referred my file to her with the thought that she might be interested in publishing an original paperback priced at one dollar. Mrs. Moore went on to say that she wanted neither to encourage me nor discourage me in this connection. She recommended that I write her my predictions whenever I had anything of national or international importance and that she would save my letters and the postmarked envelopes so that if and when the predictions came to pass, she would have documented proof of my prophecies as a basis for working with me on a book.

The letter, while gracious, deflated me. What was I going to do now? Seven years of waiting and working and hoping and praying, and now I was right back where I started.

"Where are You, God?" I cried. "Why have You forsaken me? Have I not done everything You asked? Have I not kept my faith in You, and listened to You, and made myself content and humble in the face of adversity? Where are You, God?" I repeated.

And the Voice answered, *"I have not left you, Jeanne. I will show you the way. Trust in Me, child."*

It took a few days for me to be able to pick myself up and dust myself off and start all over again.

At that point, I called Mrs. Moore in New York. "Mrs. Moore," I began after introducing myself, "there is no need to wait for years to publish my story. I already have documented evidence that my predictions have been accurate. I have affidavits. I have journals that my family and I have kept over the past seven years. Is that not sufficient proof of the fact that I am not a crackpot, and that I have a story to tell?"

A Grain of Mustard

She was patient and heard me out. Then she spoke with great tenderness. "Mrs. Gardner, believe me, I would like to help you. But I have a responsibility to my company and to our stockholders. I can't publish a book unless it has great mass market appeal. And until I am certain in my own judgment that your story has sufficient substance my conscience will not permit me to say yes."

I thanked her, and told her I would be in touch with her again.

And on March 7, 1968, I wrote Bea Moore a letter, and in it I offered some of the prophecies given to me by the Voice. I told her that the Johnson Administration would come to a close in November. I told her that Richard Nixon would be the Republican candidate, after names like Romney, Reagan, and Rockefeller were discussed and vetoed, and that Nixon would win the election by a very slim margin.

Mrs. Moore's response to my letter made it quite apparent that she was not going to make an affirmative decision about the book based upon these political prophecies. I was frustrated and, for the first time since I realized the tremendous responsibility I had inherited, I was frightened. There was no one to help me but God, and, oh, how I prayed to Him to show me the way to get the story published! The Voice repeated in strong, commanding tones that it was the time to move, but I seemed paralyzed in my efforts. Still, the name Simon & Schuster was present in every message I heard, but I couldn't find a clue as to how I might get someone there to sponsor me.

It was late May when the Voice roared angrily at me, telling me that we could wait no longer. "*The story must be told. The time is now, Jeanne, heed My word, have faith, I will show you the way.*"

In desperation, I telephoned Mrs. Moore at Simon & Schuster. "I must see you as soon as possible. I wouldn't expect you to understand how important this is to me, but I hope I can convince you that the story must be told now."

She responded with a deep sigh. "Mrs. Gardner, you couldn't have picked a more inopportune time to get in touch with me. I'm leaving for Washington Sunday to attend a booksellers' convention. I'm returning to New York Wednesday only to check in briefly at my office, then I'm leaving for a five-day trip."

I hesitated, but only for a moment. "Well," I asked, "could you find a little time to see me in Washington? I'll meet you wherever you say."

Mrs. Moore was extremely courteous, but firm. "I'd be delighted to spend some time with you in Washington, Mrs. Gardner. You can find me at the Simon & Schuster booth at the Shoreham Hotel almost any time Monday or Tuesday, but let me say this to you before you prepare to make the trip. I can promise you absolutely nothing."

I told her I understood and said that I would see her sometime Monday, June 3.

I had some difficulty with my transportation arrangements, and I began to worry and wonder whether God was still by my side. Nothing had been easy up until now, but at this moment I needed reassurance more than I'd ever needed it before.

After I checked in at my hotel, I walked over to the Shoreham Hotel to look for Mrs. Moore. When I arrived at the Simon & Schuster booth, I was told that she'd just left, but someone offered to go to look for her. I was given a chair in the corner and sat there pondering my fate. This was my last chance. It was now or never. It was my will and God's against the will of Bea Moore and her associates at Simon & Schuster. I had great faith, and as I sat there, I hoped and prayed that Mrs. Moore had faith as strong as mine. If she did, she would bend to the will of God. But how would I know? This isn't the sort of thing one asks on first meeting. Faith is a personal, precious thing to some people, a subject never to be discussed. How was I going to achieve the necessary result? My hands were moist with fear as I sat and waited to take the final step in my attempt to secure publication of our story.

My thoughts were interrupted by a smiling face leaning into mine.

"Mrs. Gardner?" she asked.

"Yes, Mrs. Moore, I'm Mrs. Gardner." It was the same face I'd seen in a vision, and I felt more comfortable almost immediately.

"First of all," she said, "let me take you around and introduce you to some of my friends and associates."

I had the feeling I was being treated like the proverbial lamb being led to slaughter. I was being prepared for a negative answer with the same cordiality I had encountered on other occasions during the past seven years. I took a deep breath, said a quiet prayer, and joined Mrs. Moore for a little tour around the exhibit to meet her people and a few from other companies. Nobody but Mrs. Moore knew who I was or what I was doing there. It was logical for them to assume I was a book buyer, and the receptiveness of each person as we were introduced gave me the impression that this was the case.

I had met ten or more men and women when I was introduced to an attractive young lady about thirty years of age. As we shook hands, I knew that God was still with me, for I felt vibrations that told me that this person needed me. As I walked down the aisle of the convention hall with Mrs. Moore, I said, "That last girl I met wants to talk to me."

"I'm sure she does, Mrs. Gardner. You have the kind of face that invites conversation and conviviality."

"But you don't understand," I countered. "She wants to talk to me about herself."

Bea Moore smiled a smile that said, "Have it your way, but I know better."

Aloud, she said to me, "I don't want to be rude, but I have an obligation to be present in our hospitality suite. I'd like to ask you to join me there, but I can't spend much time with you until dinner."

I nodded my head to indicate my full understanding. "It's perfectly all right with me. I don't drink, but I love meeting new people. I'd enjoy being there, I'm sure."

So at five-thirty we repaired to the hospitality suite up-

A Grain of Mustard

stairs, and I was graciously shown a quiet seat in the corner and given a glass of ginger ale to help me pass the time while my hostess went about the task of making other visitors feel welcome.

It wasn't long, however, before the room began to swell with booksellers and the representatives of Simon & Schuster who were attending the convention. I found myself surrounded by an interesting group of people, and as we introduced ourselves to each other, I had the opportunity to tell them why I was there. It was the first time since I'd been given the gift that I spoke of it without hesitation and with great intensity. I knew that I was facing a supreme test and that this was probably the most important night of my life. Whether it was the conviction in my voice or the fact that the Divine Power was working as hard or harder than I was, I will never know. I did feel at that time, though, that I was being very well received by the people in the room, and my confidence was returning. Perhaps I could accomplish my mission on this trip.

Before the crowd dispersed to go various places for dinner, I had strangers approaching me with questions about my gift. This let me know that the word had been passed around the large room and that people were aware and interested. My confidence mounted with each new person I met.

Finally Bea Moore returned. "Do you like Spanish food, Mrs. Gardner?" I told her I did. "Well," she said, "maybe I can't publish your story, but I can show you a nice time this evening." She left me briefly to telephone for a reservation, and once more I was torn with frustration. One moment I felt as though I were on the right track; the next moment, with one terse comment from this woman, my dream was shattered. How could I convince Bea Moore that she or someone at Simon & Schuster had to join me in my crusade?

I had no chance on the way to the restaurant. Mrs. Moore was explaining that this quaint Spanish bistro was owned by a young married couple she had known for many years and that she tried to see them whenever she was in Washington. There was no opening for me to interject my problem and to plead my case, and I had the feeling that my companion's steady stream of conversation was by design. I felt that she did not want me to regale her with my prophecies because she didn't want to hurt me by saying no again.

At the restaurant we were greeted warmly by the proprietor who ushered us to "one of the best tables in the house." The surroundings were attractive and the room bore an air of excitement and frivolity. I realized almost instantly that this was not the proper setting for a heart-to-heart talk, and my realization was confirmed when a spirited troupe of flamenco dancers began to perform right next to our table.

So I sat back and tried to enjoy my meal and the entertainment, telling myself that when the time was right, I would be given an opportunity.

A Grain of Mustard

Little did I know that God was indeed at my side, staying my words until the time that they could be more effective.

Before the end of the evening, Bea Moore and I were on a first-name basis, and while I sensed the fact that she was steeling herself against a commitment to publish my story, she wanted to let me down gently and didn't quite know how to go about it. Before alighting from the cab at my hotel, I asked her whether she would be free to look at my journals sometime the following day. She said she would like that very much, and we bade each other goodnight with the promise to get together at the exhibit on Tuesday.

chapter 13

It was a restless night for me. For more than a year the name of Bobby Kennedy had appeared in clues given to me by the Voice. I was fearful that he, like his brother Jack, would meet his death through assassination, but I did not have enough information to piece the clues together. Now, this night in Washington, Monday, June 3, 1968, I was tormented by a vision of Bobby Kennedy in a large kitchen and the Voice in crying tones telling me that Bobby would be struck by the bullet of a despot. I saw the man, a short, swarthy fellow in his twenties. I tossed and turned and tried to think of other things. I couldn't believe that this young Presidential candidate could possibly be the victim of assassination at a period in his life when he was gaining in popularity and stature. There had to be some mistake.

As daylight streamed through the blinds and I lay in the bed still fighting sleeplessness, I heard the Voice in clear, authoritative tones.

"Jeanne, write this down. Get a pencil and write this down." I had learned through the years to do as I was told,

A Grain of Mustard

because a record of these messages was all that I had to convince people of my gift. I groped in my purse and found a pencil and reached to the bedside table for a small memo pad.

There was no mistake. The assassination of Robert F. Kennedy was certain. Now I had to tell someone.

My fingers faltered as I tried to dress hurriedly. Who could I tell, and what would the reaction be?

I arrived at the Shoreham Hotel breathless and trembling, only to learn that the exhibit would not open until 10 A.M. There was nothing to do but wait.

At ten o'clock the convention hall was opened to visitors, and I hurriedly made my way to the Simon & Schuster booth. I was relieved to see Bea Moore standing beside the exhibit, and I rushed to join her.

"Bea," I blurted in the same way a child reveals a tormenting secret, "there is going to be a shooting in connection with the Presidency in the early hours tomorrow morning. It will take place in or right outside a large kitchen. There will be a High Requiem Mass in St. Patrick's Cathedral in New York and one later in Hyannisport."

Before I would say anything more, Bea grabbed my wrist and pulled me closer to her. "Jeanne," she whispered, "if you must say things like that, say them quietly. Otherwise, someone with the net may grab you."

It was plain that I wasn't being taken seriously.

"Bea," I began earnestly, "do you think I would make up a dreadful story like this? It's not a joke. I heard the Voice early this morning, and all the clues it has given me over the past year were linked together. I know this shooting will happen tomorrow morning as well as I know my own name."

"Okay, Jeanne," she said in an appeasing way, "let's get out of here and go get a cup of coffee."

"I don't want coffee," I told her frantically. "I want you to believe me! You promised to come to my room and look at my journals and affidavits that will testify to my sincerity. Will you come now?"

She looked at me for a long, difficult moment, then moved her head from side to side in resignation. "All right, Jeanne, I'll go to your room now and look at your journals." It was almost as though she were trying to spare me from revealing what I knew to anyone else for fear it might hurt me. I was beyond the point of logic, however. I knew that for me this was the eleventh hour, and I had to move decisively.

We took a shortcut from the Shoreham to my hotel, and this time I took the lead in the conversation, trying to penetrate the barrier I knew Bea Moore had established concerning my gift and the story that had to be told. It was easy to understand why she wanted no part of it. There was, after all, nothing in writing, except for the outline which had already been rejected. Somehow I had to enlist her in my cause. I had to get her to join me in my quest for national recognition, so that I could get on with my primary project, building the Cathedral.

I talked rapidly in what I hoped was a convincing man-

A Grain of Mustard

ner, and as we talked, she listened, acknowledging that she heard me by nodding her head affirmatively.

When we arrived at my room, I asked her to take a seat. "Before we begin to look at my journals, perhaps you'd like to see the notes I made this morning when the Voice spoke to me of Bobby Kennedy."

"I would like to see them," she agreed.

I stepped to the bedside table and handed her the memo pad.

Bea studied each line carefully. When she'd finished, she looked up at me, her eyes wide with interest. "I must say, Jeanne, I'm fascinated, but I'm not convinced." She hurried on, as though she had to get something off her chest.

"Jeanne," she said, "before you begin to plead your case and I am put in the position of saying no to someone as nice as you, let me tell you that I admire your courage. Let me say that I am in complete awe of a person who, in the face of overwhelming adversities, has had the patience and fortitude to carry on this difficult mission.

"But," she went on, "isn't there some other way to approach your problem? Does it have to be with these prophecies? Couldn't you initiate a fund-raising program? The idea of a Cathedral for all faiths is such a wonderful one that I can imagine you would have no difficulty in finding sponsors."

Her sincerity and her desire to spare me from hurt touched me and amused me at the same time.

"Bea," I answered, "if there were any other avenue to

reach my goal, believe me, I would be pursuing it. But there isn't. I know from my experiences over the past seven years that I must do as the Voice bids me. Here," I said, extracting one of the journals from my briefcase, "look at these records dated 1963, 1964, 1965, 1966. Scattered throughout these pages, you will see the name of Simon & Schuster many times. You will also see the name Bea. At the time I wrote your name in these pages, I had no idea who you were or how you would help me. Nevertheless, the time has come for the story to be told, and here we are sitting together, talking about it."

She flipped through the pages of the book, stopping here and there to scan the words that were written, sucking in her breath from time to time, as though she'd been pinched.

"Jeanne," she said finally with a great deal of pain in her voice, "you're convinced that I'm your answer. Believe me, I am not. You're convinced that Providence has led you to me and that I can help you. You couldn't be more wrong."

I picked up one of the notebooks she had read and dropped on the floor between us. "Look here, Bea," I implored. "Do you see where the Voice told me to go to Simon & Schuster, and I asked who would help me there, and the Voice answered 'Bea'? I asked the Voice how you would help me, and the Voice replied, 'Ability.'"

"My dear," she answered quickly, her dark eyes clouding, "I'm afraid the Voice has led you down the garden path. I am a publisher of paperback books. The only way I could help would be to persuade one of the other divisions to publish your story, and how can I do that when I'm not convinced myself that you have a story?"

I smiled at her, for the first time fully confident that my efforts would not be in vain.

"You're going to help me, Bea, whether you want to or not, whether you realize it yet or not. You're going to help me."

She shook her head in mild exasperation, then sighed, as if to say, "I give up, but not for long."

"All right, Jeanne," she said. "Let me see some more of the journals."

As I reached into the briefcase to extract another journal, my hand fell on a white plastic cross I'd carried with me. I pulled it out of the bag.

"My God, Jeanne," Bea gasped, "what's that?"

I could understand why she was startled, because the cross was not an ordinary one. Through a tiny hole in its center floated a lock of my mother's flame-red hair.

Realizing that Bea might begin to think I was a little potty, I had to tell her the story of the white cross and the hair.

This experience occurred at the tail end of my siege of housecleaning following my mother's death, and when I knew my rooms were spotless. One day a neighbor came to call, and we went to the living room for a visit over a cup of tea. As we talked, a strand of flame-red hair floated down between us and settled on the rug. A chill came over me, and I was glad when my neighbor spoke. "Jeanne," she said in an awed voice, "do you see what I see?" I told her I did, and reached over to pick up the hair. Then I excused myself for a moment and went into my bedroom. I was weak and shaken. I sat down in a chair and put my head back to compose myself. It was then that a distant Voice spoke to me: *"Jeanne, child, get your mother's white cross."*

"What white cross?" I asked out loud. I didn't know that my mother had owned such an object, let alone where it could be.

"Go to your mother's room and get the white cross, Jeanne." Like a robot, I rose from my chair, and went to my mother's room, and began opening drawers. There at the back of a drawer I found this strange white plastic cross. I say strange because of the hole in its center.

I carried the cross back to my own bedroom, sat down once more in the chair, and waited for the Voice.

"Put your mother's hair through the opening of the cross and keep it with you," the Voice said, then was silent. So I did as I was told, took a deep breath, and returned to my friend who was waiting for me. I had brought the cross with me to Washington because this trip was so important to my purpose.

Bea Moore looked at me with an expression of disbelief, but I had the feeling she wanted to believe me.

"Jeanne," she said after a moment or two, "you're an interesting composite. You're sweet, companionable, intelligent, normal, and natural. Yet there's something about you that is strange and supernatural. What is it, Jeanne?

A Grain of Mustard

Have you ever thought about the effect you have on people?"

I smiled and answered carefully. "I don't think I'm strange. Maybe this work I'm trying to accomplish has left its mark on me. Maybe I have been imbued with some magnetic quality that draws people to me. I do find that when I speak to people, they often move to get closer to me. Even as you, Bea."

She straightened up in her chair, as though I had reminded her painfully that she had come to say "No."

Bea stayed another half hour, looking through the journals, asking a question here and there, and at last came back to my notes on Bobby Kennedy.

Finally she stood up, getting ready to leave.

"I don't know what to tell you, Jeanne. I came here to give you a definite no, but I can't bring myself to do it. Give me a little time to think and talk about it with some of our people, and I'll be in touch with you again."

I took her hand to say, "Good-bye," but what I felt like saying was "Hello." I knew at that moment that I was on the threshold of victory and that Bea Moore was the person who would spearhead my campaign.

She left my room with the promise that she would call me when she got back from her trip, somewhere around the middle of June.

What I did not know at that time was that instead of returning to the convention, she canceled some appointments she'd made for the day, checked out of her hotel, and caught a plane back to New York. She told me later that she didn't know why she did what she did, but she knew instinctively that she had to get back to New York and discuss our meeting with other people in her organization.

I frittered the day away, chatting with people I'd met at the convention and seeing a couple of old friends in Washington. That afternoon, as I passed the Simon & Schuster booth, a couple of their representatives hailed me. They invited me back to their hospitality suite that evening. Having nothing else scheduled, I was delighted to accept.

Again I met new people. And each person I met I told about my message from the Voice concerning Bobby Kennedy. It was only a matter of hours now.

After dinner I returned to my hotel, but I couldn't rest. This prophecy weighed heavily on me. I had asked the Voice many times if there were something I could do to prevent this terrible thing from happening, and the Voice had answered that certain things could not be changed. Yet, being human, I suffered with this knowledge inside me.

I prepared for bed, knowing that I would not be able to close an eye. I tossed and turned and tossed and turned, looking at my watch periodically. Finally, at three-thirty, I flicked on the radio. The first words I heard were the tail-end of a news bulletin confirming what I already knew. Robert Kennedy had been shot in Los Angeles. He was critically injured. I waited for the next report to hear the details.

A Grain of Mustard

How can I explain my emotions? I was exhausted, drained of energy, spirit, thought. It isn't easy to carry something like this inside you and then see it come to pass. It's like knowing that a beloved member of one's family has a terminal illness. Everyone in the family knows the person has only a short time left. Yet when the person passes on, the shock is as great as if his death were unexpected.

I fell back on the bed and lay there wide-eyed, waiting for dawn to come.

About six-forty-five my telephone rang. It was one of the Simon & Schuster people to whom I had spoken about this tragic event. Bill Holmes was completely flabbergasted.

For the next two hours there was a steady stream of calls from the convention people to whom I had mentioned this incident before it occurred.

At nine o'clock I had still another call. This one was from Bea Moore in New York.

"Jeanne," she began in a voice that sounded as if it didn't belong to her, "I can't believe it. I know it has really happened, but I can't believe it."

"I always feel that way when a prediction becomes a reality," I assured her. "It's a very natural reaction."

"Well, you were right, Jeanne. I heard it with my own ears, and all our staff people and our visitors heard it, too. You were right." It was as though for the first time she acknowledged what I had been trying to tell her for more than three months.

"Jeanne," she went on, "I have promised you nothing,

and I can still promise you nothing. But if it is convenient for you, I would like to see you in New York at the end of next week, as soon as I get back from my trip."

I told her I'd be there at nine o'clock the following Thursday, and we said good-bye.

Were all the pieces suddenly falling into place? I wondered. Why would she not commit herself or her company? Why did it have to drag on and on and on? Wasn't she convinced that I was not a crackpot and that I was telling the truth?

I searched for the Voice to comfort me, but I had to comfort myself. I got no response. Once more I would have to wait and hope and pray.

I bathed and dressed, hardly aware of what I was doing. And again my phone rang. This time it was the young lady I had met on the convention floor the first day I came to Washington. She, too, said she'd telephoned because of the news, but she added that she would like to come to see me. As I'd told Bea Moore, this girl wanted to talk to me about herself and I wanted to help her if I could. We arranged an appointment.

When I opened the door, she stood there smiling, but with a reluctance to enter. I made a gesture with my hand. "Come in, dear. I'm glad to see you."

The girl was embarrassed. "I don't really know why I'm here," she said. "I know I wanted to talk with you, and something compelled me to come."

I invited her to sit and be comfortable. "Will you give me your hand, dear?" I asked.

A Grain of Mustard

She extended her hand, placing the back of it on my palm, and I could feel her tension.

I waited a moment, both of us silent, before I had the answer.

"You poor child," I said, with utmost confidence, "you've been worrying about something that should not give you cause to worry. You were ill a couple of months back, and you're afraid that the same thing is going to happen to you again. Is that not right?"

She nodded, "That's right," she said. "I'm worried because the doctors were unable to tell me what was wrong and consequently can give no assurance that it won't happen again."

"I can tell you what was wrong." I watched her eyes grow dark with intensive interest. "An air bubble burst near your brain. Be thankful, child, that it happened, because that saved your life. But have no fear, it will not happen again." She sat there, surprised. I was as surprised as she. The Voice had directed me, had given me the answer; I couldn't have done it alone.

Tears filled her eyes, but she gathered her composure quickly. "You've just seen me through a nightmare, Jeanne," she said. Then she told me her story.

"A couple of months ago I arrived at my office in a trancelike state. I didn't know where I was or how I got there; I was completely out of this world. The people who work with me noticed that I was in a daze and called a doctor to come over as quickly as possible. I was rushed to the hospital and experienced two seizures on the way over.

For days I was subjected to every conceivable test for brain tumor, epilepsy, and the like, yet there was no concrete diagnosis. Every day since then I've wondered whether this dreadful thing will happen to me again."

"Believe me, young lady, it will not happen again," I assured her. "And I'm glad you came to talk to me."

"You're glad!" she chided. "What do you think I am? You've taken a tremendous burden from me, and I cannot thank you enough. Tell me if there is anything I can ever do for you." I shook her hand with the promise that I would call on her if I could think of anything.

I returned to Elkins that day, saddened by the Bobby Kennedy incident, but satisfied that I was on the way to achieving my goal. My family was glad to see me, and I was glad to see them. It seemed as though I'd been away a lifetime—so much had happened.

That next week I stayed busy at home, fixing food that my family would be able to prepare easily when I left for New York on what I hoped was the final lap of my seven-year journey.

Air transportation being very uncertain out of Elkins, I decided to travel to New York on the train. After finding my place, and checking in at my seat, I made my way to the dining car to have my dinner.

I was served quickly, and as I sat there eating and thinking about what I would do with my time in New York, the Voice began to speak. I leaped from my table as if I'd been shot from a cannon. I knew the steward must have thought I was out of my mind.

A Grain of Mustard

"Please don't take my food away," I told him as I passed him, almost knocking him down. "I'll be right back."

I raced to my seat to get a notebook and hurried back to my table in the dining car, where I began to write feverishly. I had already missed the first part of the message.

Much to my surprise, the message I received was not for me, but for Bea Moore, whom I was on my way to see in New York.

The Voice talked of her childhood, how He had watched her from above. The Voice told her of her great heart, her kindness to people, and asked her to help me in this great work I was attempting to perform. I was a little embarrassed as I read over what I had written. It was like reading someone else's mail, but I couldn't help it. I had done simply what I had learned to do over the past seven years: listened and recorded.

After checking in at my hotel, I made my way over to Simon & Schuster. It was a sultry day in the middle of June. I tried not to think about the heat but to concentrate on how I could convince the people at Simon & Schuster that my story and the story of my mother, my aunts, and my grandmother had to be told.

I walked into Bea Moore's office with a smile on my face and a prayer in my heart. After shaking hands and exchanging a few pleasantries, I related the incident that had occurred in the dining car on my way up from Elkins and handed her the notebook to read.

She took the notebook, placed it on her desk, and shot me a sidelong glance, as if to say, "What are you giving me?" Then she put on her reading glasses very slowly and thoughtfully and lowered her eyes to the page before her.

Her reading was very deliberate. It seemed as though she were never going to finish, or wanted not to finish for fear she would have to take up conversation with me again. I waited silently, nervously, prayerfully.

Finally, rubbing her arm as if trying to overcome a chill, she looked up at me.

"Jeanne," she said, looking straight into my eyes, "let us say that Simon & Schuster would agree to publish your story—do you have anyone who can put it together for you?"

I told her I did not. I reminded her of what had happened earlier when I'd asked the professional writer to write my story in capsule form for the Editorial Board of Simon & Schuster, and how I'd been turned down.

"Well, Jeanne," she went on patiently, "you must understand that we have to have a manuscript in order to produce a book. And the way the story should be told is the way you tell it. So you have to have a person to write it who knows your ways, your manner of speaking, to whom you can talk and who can translate for the reading public in your style. Have you in your travels met anyone like that, Jeanne—someone who is sympathetic to you and your project, who will put his heart and soul into it as you are doing?"

I smiled. "Yes," I said, "I know someone exactly like you've described." Then I sat back and looked at her steadfastly.

A Grain of Mustard

Her mouth fell open, her eyes grew wide, and she appeared to be speechless for a moment. She stood up and made signs, throwing her hands into the air wildly. "Jeanne," she sputtered, "you don't mean . . ." and the words trailed off as she pointed to herself.

"That's exactly who I mean," I told her. "You're going to write my book for me. I think I've known that for almost five years now: I had the name Bea, but I didn't know who Bea was. I'm positive now. It's you, and you're going to write my story."

"Oh, no, Jeanne," she protested, "this time you must be wrong. My work is administrative, editorial, but not creative. I can't write a book. I've never written a book, nor have I ever had an inclination to write a book."

"But you're going to do it this time," I told her with complete assurance because, for the first time in all the years I'd been visiting Simon & Schuster, I felt an inner force that made me confident.

Bea excused herself and went into another office where she remained for about twenty minutes. When she returned, she stood before me, and in the voice of a person who is slowly but surely dropping into quicksand, she pleaded, "Jeanne, let's get out of this place and go to lunch."

All through luncheon she avoided talking about the book. We did talk about my grandmother, my mother, my family, my mother's songs, how I met Governor Hughes. Every question she asked was a searching one. She seemed to be weighing every answer.

We lingered over luncheon about two hours. Then we returned to her office.

Once inside, Bea turned to me. "Jeanne," she said, "I believe in you. But I don't have time to put your story together. Running my division is all the responsibility I can handle, and then some. In addition, I have my husband and our home to think about. Writing a book takes time, thought, creative effort. I'd like to help you out, Jeanne, but I just can't."

This time I couldn't be stopped. "You're going to do it, Bea. I know you want to do it, and you're going to do it. I've never been more certain of anything in my life. And you'll have the help of God. He'll be at your side. He'll make it go easier than you think it will."

My assurance of God's help seemed to impress her. She reflected quietly for quite some time, turning her chair so that I could not read her face.

"Jeanne," she said finally, "do you own a tape recorder?"

"Yes," I told her, "I do."

"If I were to write a very definitive outline for a book, based on what you have told me the times we've been together," she went on, "would you be able to stick to that outline and send the tapes to me?"

"Of course," I told her confidently, hopeful that she was coming over to my side at last.

"Jeanne," she concluded almost in a whisper, "I can promise you nothing other than the fact that I will do my best to put your story together in readable form. But before I can offer you a contract, I have to speak to the pub-

A Grain of Mustard

lisher of another of our divisions. Excuse me a few moments more."

She left the office and returned in less than ten minutes. "Okay, Jeanne, we've got a deal. Trident Press, a hardcover imprint, is willing to add your story to its list." With that, she raised her head toward heaven. "God help me," she whispered, and I knew He would.

That is how this story came into being. I created tapes, sticking to the outline I was furnished as well as I could. There were endless phone calls between New York and Elkins, sleepless nights in both places, days that I spent at Bea Moore's home while we tried to smooth out details that she was not able to grasp from my tapes.

Now the story has been told, and it is in God's hands. Whether or not the book becomes a success depends on the people who read it, their interest in God's work and the very small part I played in it.

For you who have finished reading, I have a prayer. I pray that you have learned from my experience that you, too, can witness miracles if you will only open your eyes and your heart. You can move mountains, too, if you will develop faith, even the size of a mustard seed.

God bless you, one and all.

chapter 14

I HAVE had many questions asked of me concerning the Voice and my visions. I, myself, have asked many questions of the Voice for my own satisfaction as well as for the satisfaction of those who wanted answers from me. One thing I would like to make clear. This power which I have been given to envisage incidents that will occur in the future was not given to me as entertainment. I did nothing consciously to strengthen it, other than to recognize that it was real, and to acknowledge to myself that I had to pay heed. The primary purpose of my having the power of prophecy is to attract attention to me, so that people will listen.

I am not a preacher. I have no desire to become one. But, I have assumed this task and I know I must see it through to fulfillment.

Here are some of the most common questions asked of me through the years:

Q. Are there really such things as flying saucers?
A. Very definitely.

A Grain of Mustard

Q. Are these vehicles piloted by creatures from other planets?
A. They are. There is life on other planets, not with the same physical characteristics as earth people, but with high intellect.

Q. Why do these creatures not attack us?
A. They are curious; they do not wage warfare.

Q. There is a lot of talk about germicidal warfare. Is such a thing possible?
A. Even now, there is something in the air that pricks the skin, causing the victims to rub the affected area. This will ultimately have its effect in weakening the populace.

Q. There is a lot of talk among the so-called prophets that part of the country as we know it will be removed. Do you believe this?
A. You must understand that I believe only what I am told by the Voice. I have no desire to seek outside verification, because I trust in the Voice. I am told by Him that unless we, as a nation, restore our faith in God, by His great hand He will destroy our land. There will be ice slides from the North, great weather changes, tidal waves, earthquakes, land cave-ins. Because of the adversities I have had to face in my life thus far, I am willing to believe all of it. Without faith, I would have been a poor, miserable, self-pity-

ing creature with no accomplishment in life, probably blaming God for my failure instead of blaming myself.

Q. What does this Voice sound like to you?
A. It comes in many ways. Sometimes it is breathless, happy; sometimes it is husky, grieving; other times, it wails and cries and repeats the same thing over and over. The last is always true when it speaks of tragedy or death.

Q. Do you think it is one person or thing?
A. That's difficult for me to answer. Sometimes it tells me "I am the Star of Nazareth," which would lead me to believe it is Jesus. Sometimes it says, "I am the Great I Am," or "I am Alpha and Omega, the beginning and the end," and "I sent my only son," which makes me think it is God. As far as I am concerned, it could be either or both, and I am interested and dedicated equally.

Q. We are told to love our neighbor, learn brotherhood, and the like. Yet animals are more civil to each other than man is to man. How do you explain that?
A. I have been asked that many times, and I have pondered it myself. This is the answer I have received from the Voice:
You ask why animal seems more civil than man.
It's been this way, Jeanne, since the world began.

A Grain of Mustard

You see, when Eve took the apple within,
She brought to the world the wages of sin.
By tempting her with the apple, old Lucifer, the devil,
Brought upon the earth corruption and upheaval.
Then this was the beginning of temptation in life
That was soon to fall on many, causing universal strife.
I then had to thrust these two from my Garden fair,
And they had to find themselves an unanointed lair.
The first to be slain by their lustful act
Was Abel who was killed by Cain many centuries back.
Listen, man's been killing man all the way from the beginning,
And will until the end of time, the end of all men's sinning.
There are kings of now, there were kings of yore;
They've lived like kings, but they will no more;
For all through the years these kings in lustful rages
Were cruel and murdered, now some must pay the wages.

Do you understand me, child? I speak. Listen. Heed me well.

I have said that in the beginning I gave to the world a beautiful garden which was called Eden. I told the woman named Eve not to eat of the apple of Good and Evil. But the voice of Satan tempted her, and she entered the Garden and could not resist temptation.

I cast Eve and the man called Adam from Me. I cast them into a world with corruption and hate to follow. It was like a disease. Greed was the result. Greed overtook all the people who thought of themselves as kings, men who believed they were more powerful than I. I knew then that I had to do something. So I sent my Son into the world as a little babe in the manger to save the world from this greed, from hate, malice, jealousy. But this was not enough. Incensed by fear of losing power, they crucified my Son. They nailed Him on a cross between two thieves to die a death of horror.

Do you think He wanted to die, Jeanne? No, I say to you, never! But He did as I had willed it, and I took care of Him as He hung there in the sun until those who watched Him heard Him say, "Alas, now all is done."

But He arose in three days, hoping that this miracle might save the world from sin. But it hasn't helped, for man has either forgotten or has never believed in Him. This temptation for power, this greed and hate has never stopped and it will not stop till My Son comes back again. I sent Him first as a Savior. Now I send Him as a King. This King will be humble, will put an end to man's killing man, for all men are the same to Me, regardless of the way they look or how they show Me their love.

Your people talk of dumb animals. This again is cruel. These creatures are not dumb. They have more love, more compassion, than man has for man. Man is still paying the price for killing My Son; man suffereth still from that same lust for power and will until the end of time. But remember, child, man killed My Son, not an animal. Oh, I have given man many chances to free himself, but he has denied each one. Animals know not of greed, hate, jealousy . . . only of survival and of protecting their offspring. Man is

A Grain of Mustard

never satisfied. He is ever seeking more, more, more, and with this lust he is flanked by my enemies: hate, malice, envy.

Do you understand, child? Do you see why man continues to kill man? One small sin, the act of Eve, has multiplied a billionfold and has brought strife and turmoil to all who dwell on earth.

> Hark, I say unto you, all killing will have ended;
> I will hear praise from everyone
> When I send you back the greatest King
> From here on high, My Son.

Q. Why do you think you were chosen for this work of building a Cathedral?

A. I don't know, honestly. Certainly it is nothing that I would have selected for myself. I could have been content forevermore simply being the best wife and mother I knew how to be. You have only to look at me or to talk with me to realize that I am not "equipped" to build a Cathedral. I couldn't have done it unless I were guided. Maybe it is because I am a simple being, one who would listen, that I was chosen for this work.

Q. What has the Voice told you about our war in Vietnam and future wars?

A. We will have a Third World War, but not before we have war on five fronts.

Q. Who will be our enemies and who will be our allies?
A. I would have to decline being specific, although I do have some word on this. I do not want to influence anyone's thinking. This I can offer as a word of caution. Some who appear to be our friends speak with forked tongues. When the time draws nearer, you will see that many whom we have befriended will turn on us and we will be left with few allies.

Q. If there is a God, why does He not stop wars, killing, rioting, and the like?
A. I have asked this of the Voice, and He has answered. It is up to the people of the world to redeem themselves. Unfortunately, many of the good suffer for the wicked. But unless the majority of the people of the world awaken to the fact that greed, avarice, and coveting lead only to destruction, we will then all be destroyed. I guess you could say it's a matter of teamwork, not a matter of winning but how the game is played. No man is an island, neither is a country or a continent today. We have to learn to live together or to die together.

Q. Do you have any idea when we will have a Third World War?
A. I have no more idea of when that will happen than I do any other disaster, unless I am told specifically by the Voice. God's time, as I understand it, is com-

A Grain of Mustard

pletely different from man's time. Perhaps that is just as well.

Q. You are constantly saying, "Have faith," "Develop faith." How can someone who thinks scientifically, someone who calls a spade a spade, just out of the clear blue develop faith?

A. I don't think it can be done simply by making up your mind to do it. You have to be shown the way. It's an easy matter in these times to be shown the way. Look around you. If you don't like what you see, if you think that the greed of nations and the human destruction in our own country caused by man pitting himself against man are outrageous, try prayer. Don't ask that wars cease overnight or that rioting and protesting come to a halt quickly. I can tell you it won't happen. Ask that your own faith be strengthened and that you, yourself, be shown the way to peace and brotherhood. If enough of us do this, we'll have no problem of this sort.

Q. Mrs. Gardner, do you really believe all that you talk about, or are you some kind of a propagandist for religion?

A. This question is asked me by more than half the people with whom I speak. I suppose it is justified, because some of the things I say, which have been given to me by the Voice, seem farfetched. Yet if I am to believe it at all, I know I must believe all of it. I do believe. I would not insist that anyone I have met believe as I do. Hopefully, when some of the miracles I have talked about take place, many of their own volition will seek greater faith. I hope most people will not wait for miracles, but will be a part of the miracles.